Praise for *I Just Need Time to Think!*

Once I started reading, I couldn't stop. *I Just Need Time to Think!* is fabulous. Mark's book is permission, if not a direct order, to take your time, go slow, absorb what you hear, ponder what you read and analyze what you see as thinking creatures in God's magnificent world.

> Lori Borgman, columnist, speaker and author of *The Death of Common Sense and Profiles of Those Who Knew Him.*

A favorite professor of mine once said his purpose was to help his students think. By that standard, Mark Eckel is a consummate Christian educator. He is among the absolute best at provoking thought in the Christian reader, and this treasure of essays is wonderful example. Get ready for an exciting adventure. *I Just Need Time to Think!* will not only entertain, provoke, amuse, and inspire you. It will help you grow.

> Dr. David Claerbaut, founder of www.faithandlearningforum.com, is author of 15 books. *What is True? A Defense of the Christian Faith* is most recent (Kindle).

In our attention-challenged age of Twitter, the soundbite and the video clip, these essays by Mark Eckel challenge us to slow down and savor the abundant gifts that God offers in creation. For the health and well-being of humanity, indeed all creation, we need to cultivate practices of study and marvel. *I Just Need Time to Think!* is a carefully written work directing us there.

> C. Christopher Smith, Editor of *The Englewood Review of Books* and co-author of *Slow Church: Cultivating Community in the Patient Way of Jesus.*

Mark Eckel has spent his whole life teaching people how to live from a biblical worldview. In his new book *I Just Need Time to Think!*, Mark introduces us to the concept of reflective study and shows us how to deeply think about the things that truly matter.

Hugh Whelchel, Executive Director, The Institute for Faith, Work and Economics
Author of *How Then Should We Work?: Rediscovering the Biblical Doctrine of Work*

Through a series of witty, humorous and moving essays, Mark Eckel's new book will challenge readers to think in radically new ways about what it means to be a serious student of the life of the mind. Reflecting on topics such as study, place, reflection, reading, and retreat Mark gives readers fresh insights in skills critical for a life well led.

Rob Wingerter, Founder and President of Mahseh Retreat Center

Jesus said, "Love the Lord your God with all your...mind." Mark does just that in *I Just Need Time To Think!* His text is my tool for reflective retreat and study -- and what a great tool it is: enlightening, challenging, and encouraging. Make it your guide and it will be life-transforming.

Dr. Tommy Kiedis, Senior Pastor, Spanish River Church, Boca Raton, Florida

Like the well-worn pages of my grandmother's Bible, each topic has been so obviously crafted into being by years of what the book is calling us back to: reflective interactions with one another concerning the truths offered up by the Biblical texts. Set against our unreflective age, this collection of Dr. Mark Eckel's passionately worked-out themes commend themselves to us by the turned-up edges of the thoughts they convey.

Richard L Klopp, VP Africa Partnerships, Blood: Water Mission, Water for Good

April 2014

Blessings on your work for King & Kingdom

I Just Need Time to Think!

Reflective Study as Christian Practice

Peace

Mark D. Eckel

WestBow
PRESS
A DIVISION OF THOMAS NELSON

WestBow Press books may be ordered through booksellers or by contacting:

WestBow Press
A Division of Thomas Nelson
1663 Liberty Drive
Bloomington, IN 47403
www.westbowpress.com
1 (866) 928-1240

Because of the dynamic nature of the Internet, any web addresses or links contained in this book may have changed since publication and may no longer be valid. The views expressed in this work are solely those of the author and do not necessarily reflect the views of the publisher, and the publisher hereby disclaims any responsibility for them.

Any people depicted in stock imagery provided by Thinkstock are models, and such images are being used for illustrative purposes only. Certain stock imagery © Thinkstock.

Scripture quotations are from The Holy Bible, English Standard Version® (ESV®), copyright © 2001 by Crossway, a publishing ministry of Good News Publishers. Used by permission. All rights reserved.

ISBN: 978-1-4908-1938-9 (sc)
ISBN: 978-1-4908-1939-6 (hc)
ISBN: 978-1-4908-1937-2 (e)

Library of Congress Control Number: 2013922099

Printed in the United States of America.

WestBow Press rev. date: 12/20/2013

Contents

Preface

The walk around the lake is four and a half miles. Every day I read fifty to sixty pages as I traversed the route. I would stop and chat with folks along the way, often answering the question, "How can you read and walk at the same time?!" Pencil in hand, I would take notes in the margins of the books I read during the one hour commute.

Lake Bruce in Kewanna, Indiana provided my walking circuit where I served for two years as director of the Mahseh Center (mahseh.org). Rob and Deb Wingerter, patrons of Mahseh, asked me to procure books for the library, provide oversight for retreat-study groups, offer resident teaching, and supply writing around Christian themes of retreat and study. The fifty-two essays in this volume create both a foundation and invitation to Christians for the spiritual disciplines of retreat and study. Most of the writing in this book originated during my Mahseh ministry.

Reflective study as Christian practice, the sub-title for this volume, rises from the opportunity we create to retreat; withdrawing from the normal pace of life for a time. My local church small group participated in thoughtful learning. Recent college graduates met regularly with me for study-retreat sessions. College groups to church groups to school groups to individuals shared in occasions to learn together.

For over 30 years I have taught students, kindergarten through doctoral studies, to do one thing: *think biblically*. In many ways this volume is the *ethos*, the Christian educational culture, to which I have been committed. Student stories punctuate these pages. I have breathed the same classroom air with colleagues whose influence is also present here. The ever present mantra "Do not believe anything I say but search Scripture to see if it is so" echoes in each essay. Teaching people *what* to think has never interested me; teaching them *how* to think is my ever-present passion.

Time spent in Christian reflection must be premised upon serious commitment to read, ponder, write, and contribute. Unfortunately, some Christian contributions are built upon cultural conditions rather than biblical bases. *I Just Need Time to Think!* is an encouragement to set aside time to Christianly consider before we contribute. Thought without practice is dead. But practice without thought kills, reminiscent of Jesus' oft-stated words to the Pharisees, "Have you never read in The Scriptures . . . ?"

My walk may be around a lake or a classroom, but the focus on taking time for reflective study remains the same. May The Father who plans, The Son who provides, and The Spirit who protects receive all glory for the opportunities The Church takes for reflective study.

Mark D. Eckel, ThM PhD
Professor of Leadership, Education & Discipleship
Capital Seminary and Graduate School
Washington, D.C.

Foreword

On some mornings, especially with just a bit of morning fog, our Lancaster Bible College campus looks like a picture postcard. If you come on our campus in late spring or early summer, you soon discover a stunning array of perennial flowers in bloom. Perennial flowers are flowers that return each year.

Some ideas are like that. They are perennial in nature. No matter how long we live and how many generations come and go, perennial ideas endure. Dr. Mark Eckel captures those perennial ideas in this book and draws his reader to consider them anew. Mark Eckel is a perennialist educator. He is committed to the great books, great ideas, and profound concepts that shape human history and form the mind. Mark calls us to reconsider these ideas in a world where technology, rapid change, and misinformation can sometimes paralyze, isolate, and deaden our minds.

When you read this book, be ready to think. Mark pushes us to exercise our God-given intellect as he provokes us to look beyond culturally accepted perspectives and modern conventional wisdom. By pulling us back to the Word of God, he challenges readers to think, read, and renew our minds.

Beware! You will not read this book without reacting. Mark isn't looking for agreement, he is looking for response. He is provoking his readers to react, to process, to reflect. Throughout the book, I found myself thinking, "That is a fresh thought" or "I haven't considered that perspective before." This book will engage you as you ponder ideas through the lens of this biblical thinker who isn't afraid to dare his readers to ask hard questions and to seek biblical answers.

At times you will disagree, but that is perfectly fine. Mark would like that. He is, of course, first a teacher. His vocation has been one of influencing, informing, and sometimes infuriating students as he has pressed them to consider life and learning beyond surface-level considerations. Seventeen years of teaching high school students, several more years in higher education teaching college students, and still more years teaching masters students and even doctoral students, have made Mark an effective classroom teacher and communicator. He knows how to get students to engage in learning. In this book, his skill as a storyteller, his ability to draw on cultural illustrations and his breadth of knowledge all serve to fuel personal reflection page by page.

Peter W. Teague, EdD
President
Lancaster Bible College (lbc.edu)
Capital Seminary and Graduate School (bible.edu)

Introduction

She emailed me from Maryland. My friend was a Christian schoolteacher, teaching junior high science. "Almost every day, I am accosted with the question, 'Why do we have to study *this*?'" she began. "You know how that nasal, high-pitched whine sounds. I hate hearing it, but I don't know how to answer it." Her cry resonates from teachers everywhere. "Do I even know why I am studying this subject?"

That Sunday, I asked my wife, Robin, to take notes as we drove in the car. She recorded twelve reasons to study subjects from a Christian point of view. I sent the list to my friend. Here is part of the response I remember from a long email I received from her a week later:

> I couldn't wait until they asked the question again. I did not have to wait long. It was a Wednesday. We had just begun to discuss the periodic table. I called on a raised hand in the back of the room. There it was. In full nasal whine, the student repeated the dreaded question. I began to read your list. By the time I got to number four, students began to cry out, "Okay! Okay! We get it!" in a vain attempt to stop the onslaught. You know what I did? I kept reading! By the time I got to number eight, I heard audible groans emanating from various individuals. When I finished number twelve, I looked around; every head was down on its desk. I smiled and asked the class, "Are there any questions?"
>
> One hearty soul bravely inquired in a respectful tone, "Do we have to hear the list anymore?"

I put a superficial frown on my face to respond, "I think it might be best if we read one of these statements every day."

From time immemorial, students have asked the question, "Why do we have to learn *this?*" God's Word makes the answer clear in twelve statements.

1. If this is God's world, He made it, and it is important to Him; it should be important to us (Genesis 1; 1 Chronicles 29:11; Nehemiah 9:6; Psalms 33:6–11, 50:9–12, 89:11).
2. If creation praises God for His works, then we should praise God for His creation (Psalms 19, 104, 148).
3. We honor, magnify, and glorify God for who He is—Creator of all (Ecclesiastes 12:1; Isaiah 40:26, 42:5, 44:24, 45:7, 18; Amos 4:13; John 1:3; Acts 7:5; Romans 1:25; 1 Corinthians 8:6; Ephesians 3:9; 1 Peter 4:19).
4. If all knowledge comes from Jesus, then we are responsible for that knowledge (Colossians 2:2–3—cf. 1:9; 2:4, 8).
5. We are responsible to grow in Jesus' knowledge (Ephesians 1:15–23; Philemon 1:9–11; Colossians 1:9–10).
6. We are responsible to develop biblical, critical thinking skills (Proverbs 2:1–6; Colossians 2:8; Hebrews 5:11–14). Wisdom is how we better understand the world (Proverbs 8).
7. As creatures responsible to the Creator, we are given responsibilities to rule the creation (Genesis 1:28, 2:5, 15, 19–20; Psalm 8:5–8).
8. God has created the earth for human benefit (Psalm 115:16; Isaiah 45:12).
9. Even unbelievers ponder what God has done in His creation (Psalm 64:9, 65:8, 66:4, 67:2, 7), which should be the believers' response (Psalm 111:2).
10. We should thank God for the various gifts given to people, whatever they are and however they may benefit others (Romans 12; 1 Corinthians 12; Ephesians 4:11–12; 1 Peter 4:10–11).
11. We give God glory in everyday living about everything (Psalm 115:1; 1 Corinthians 10:31; Colossians 3:23).
12. *Satisfaction, appreciation,* and *thankfulness* make up the most important SAT test we will ever take (Deuteronomy 8:10–20). To

be ungrateful for the gifts given to us is to reject the One who has given them (Romans 1:21). We ought to give thanks for all things (Ephesians 5:20; 1 Thessalonians 5:18), since He has given everything for us to enjoy (1 Timothy 6:17).

Satisfaction, appreciation, and thankfulness are intangible benefits to study and are gained through reflection. Taking time to consider our studies and having the proper opportunity to ponder what we learn are as important as the concepts themselves. Study without occasion to understand and opening to comprehend leaves study meaningless.

For years, I have utilized the Hebraic concept of *selah* to encourage reflection with my students. *Selah* is a word that appears often in the Psalms. The concept includes but does not exhaust thoughts such as *stop, think, ponder, meditate, consider, contemplate,* and *deliberate.* Instead of requiring hundreds of pages read, students were asked to read forty, musing over ideas within specific parameters. Observation, question, stimulation, tension, compare-contrast, or agree-disagree were all possible responses to *selah.* "I had never thought of that before," "This idea bothered me," or "The page prompted me to write" were introductory clauses that made me smile.

Kemille was forever thankful to be introduced to something new yet exciting. Lachelle launched herself headlong into the hard work of digging for detail. Theron taped classes, took copious notes, and reproduced every classroom session in a Word document. Patricia came to my office to ask questions for an hour about what she had read. Kevin pored over words, phrases, or sentences, all gold nuggets in his search for wisdom. Janelle always wanted an answer to "Why?" David pressed for more information. Haung Dau made sure of every word to make sure he understood every concept. Floyde's questions were ever honest, Howard was forever concerned with praxis, and Katie's focus on correlation made sure her thinking tied directly to her reading. Students' reflections could be multiplied many times over in a multiplicity of ways.

Every chapter on study in *I Just Need Time to Think!* is immediately followed by a chapter on reflection. Each essay in each chapter establishes a biblical basis for why Christian study and reflection are imperative. *I Just Need Time to Think! Reflective Study as Christian Practice* is an encouragement to Christ-followers everywhere to honor Christ with our learning. Study should not be separated from our need to retreat. Discipline in education at times necessitates holiday to make it happen. Reading demands our reflection. Obstacles to study indicate we need to keep on walking toward that goal. Our path of learning means that a place to study is indispensable. Each of fifty essays orbits around the theme that taking time to think, joined with reflective study, should be our normal practice as Christians.

The serious student of Scripture—from the home school family to the Christian school faculty to the passionate Sunday school teacher to anyone committed to the practice of reflective study—will find encouragement to think. From teenager to mature adult, from pastoral staff to parishioner, from man to woman, and from those with few opportunities to those with many, *I Just Need Time to Think! Reflective Study as Christian Practice* will nurture necessary, thoughtful responses to the inevitable question "Why do I have to learn *this?*"

Study: Habits of the Heart

True education builds from the inside out.

"I'm afraid I will be successful at things that don't matter," a Christian man began. "I want to learn what will change the core of my being. My accomplishments as a person are worth little if my focus is on the fiscal and physical." It is not often that one hears such honesty. Human cultures everywhere focus on the external. What a person produces makes her what she is. Prestige is given to measurable accomplishment. The unseen is unvalued. Building the internal, from the inside out, creates a strong personal core.

Alexis de Tocqueville, the French sociologist, visited America at the beginning of the nineteenth century to see what made the fledgling country distinctive. De Tocqueville discovered a population that lived life based on unwavering religious principles. He referred to these internal barometers as "habits of the heart."

By contrast, individuals and organizations today focus on what is referred to as values. *Values* can be characterized as arbitrary (individual or institutional choice reigns), acceptable (current conditions or culture dictate what matters most), and authority (tied to the consumer, "what sells" is often the basis for *values*). I refer to *values* as a weak word. We need strong terms that clearly designate our intentions.

A better word is *virtue,* which describes "conformity to a standard or right." In church history, Augustine, Aquinas, and others subscribed to justice, prudence, temperance, and courage as key *virtues*. God has infused virtue with an ultimate good in sight that is not inflated by human pride. There is a desire to build good people from the inside out. Virtues are what de Tocqueville meant by "habits of the heart."

Those who study literature know that a life is best built from the inside out. Harold Brodkey wrote, "As a rule, a writer and a book or a poem are no good if the writer is essentially unchanged morally after having written it. ... Writing always tends toward a kind of moral stance—this is because of the weight of logic and of truth in it."[1]

Sven Birkets exclaims, "Literature remains the unexcelled means of interior exploration and connection-making."[2] Virtuous stories build a person's interiority. Vigen Guroian's "Why Should Businessmen Read Great Literature"[3] is an essay that inverts the importance of the external over the internal. A more succinct reason why novels establish ethics in any reader will be hard to find.

Some commit their standards to current cultural conventions—arbitrary values of the moment. Virtue, on the other hand, depends on eternal patterns. Virtue is based upon the personal, eternal Creator. Jesus' claims establish the Christian worldview on Himself.[4]

A few years ago, a Christian school asked me to rewrite its handbook. Developing the "habits of the heart" theme, I crafted a number of objectives that are drawn from an external source for an internal focus. The first four read as follows:

1. The triune, eternal, personal Creator brought into reality a structured, patterned, ordered world that is both reliable and knowable, given for human good.[5]
2. We help to develop habits in children that are directed toward what God has established as creational law—the way life is to be properly lived. *Virtue* is the proper ordering of one's life after God-ordained ends. *Virtue* is the development of these good habits. *Virtue* is creating a disposition toward the good. To do good is first to think and be good.[6]
3. God has created us for Himself. The proper response to God and His world is tied to a proper relationship with Him and His creation.[7]
4. We are about building the interior life of a child with the help of the Spirit under authority of the Word of God. Some refer to these as spiritual disciplines.[8]

"I don't want to be successful in things that don't matter." My friend's words still ring in my ears. He wanted to set aside the valuing processes established by a pagan culture. I constantly ask myself these questions:

1. Does this thing have an eternal focus?
2. Does this activity promote virtuous living?
3. Does what I read build internal fortitude?
4. Do I practice justice, prudence, temperance, and courage as the framework of my being?
5. Is what I see always seen through what is unseen?

Virtues should trump values. Otherwise, weak words make for a weak life.

Study: Intellectuals in Love

Tell me what you love, and I will tell you who you are.

The story is told by Charles Hodge, famous twentieth-century theologian, of the most popular professor at Princeton in his day. Philip Lindsay was a man actively sought by many universities in the mid-Atlantic states to be their president. Hodge explains, "Lindsay told our class that we would find one of the best preparations for death was a thorough knowledge of the Greek grammar. This was his way of telling us that we ought to do our duty.[9]

"Tell me what you love, and I will tell you what you are" is the famous connection between knowing and doing. A. G. Sertillanges continues the idea: "Love is the beginning of everything in us ... Truth visits those who love her, who surrender to her, and this love cannot be without virtue."[10] Submission to truth shows one's affection.

We should all be intellectuals in some measure. Famed American pastor-scholar Jonathan Edwards preached to his flock that study is "not only for the instruction of ministers and men of learning; but for the instruction of all men, of all sorts, learned and unlearned, men, women, and children."[11]

Christian learning for Christian duty must be linked with Christ's passion. B. B. Warfield explains, "There is no mistake more terrible than to suppose that activity in Christian work can take the place of depth of Christian affections ... the foundation stone of your piety. ... That is to be found, of course, in your closets, or rather in your hearts, in your private religious exercises, and in your intimate religious aspirations."[12]

Love for God's law, testimonies, commandments, precepts, and words[13] in Psalm 119 is more than emotion. Hebrews placed feelings in the background while love's commitment took the foreground.[14] To "love God's law" was intensively[15] intentional for the believer. Psalm 119:47 complements the love of the study of Scripture with "delight" in Scripture.[16] Festive, exultant[17] enthusiasm[18] is present as the writer cheers heaven's book. The resulting pleasure from such teaching is a word such as *bibliophile*—book lover.

Two decades ago, I first met the efforts of some to squelch the growing love of study. Craig, one of my most passionate students, was told by some on a ministry trip that his desire to spend time reading was self-centered. *Who would want to quell this young man's burgeoning desire to grow?* I thought. Edwards reminds us, "So there can be no love without knowledge. It is not according to the nature of the human soul, to love an object which is entirely unknown. The heart cannot be set upon an object of which there is no idea in the understanding. The reasons which induce the soul to love must first be understood before they can have a reasonable influence on the heart."[19]

Great joy is gained from study and its application to real-world living. Psalm 119:18 was often my classroom prayer: "Open my eyes that I might see wonderful things in Your law!" The great teacher of preachers, Haddon Robinson, called for "evangelistic scholars"[20] to put feet to head knowledge. And anyone who wants to motivate a classroom need read Howard Hendricks *Teaching to Change Lives*[21] at least once a year to watch the seamlessness of study with joy. The Christian teacher requires a passionate love for truth. Samuel Solivan proposed the term *orthopathos* (literally, straight love) linking *orthodoxy* (straight teaching) with *orthopraxis* (straight living). Delight and truth must hold hands walking down the road of duty.[22]

So, Lindsay was right: a theologian's best preparation for death means the study of Greek grammar. Love of study (whatever field in God's creation ignites our passions) shows one's love for God. John W. Peterson expressed it best in a forgotten hymn *A Student's Prayer*. The first stanza summarizes why intellectuals are in love.[23]

> God, the all wise, and Creator of the human intellect,
> Guide our search for truth and knowledge, all our thoughts
> and ways direct.
> Help us build the towers of learning that would make us
> wise, astute,
> On the rock of Holy Scripture: Truth revealed and absolute.

Study: My Mom and Her Camera

Is it possible to say why we exist without remembering why?

"You'll be happy that I'm taking these pictures someday!" My mom whips out her camera whenever the family is together. And I *am* grateful that she has been so insistent over all these years. Mom makes her own greeting cards, always with a print of a picture she has taken. My study has many of the mementos Mom has sent over the years for any celebratory day I could recount. Benjamin Patton agrees:

> Every family has a story, and every member's story is worth preserving—certainly for the living family, even more so for future generations. Experiencing history through the lens of another person's life can offer unexpected insight into your own. It gets you to think: What sort of mark will *I* make? How will *I* be remembered? ... Annie Dillard tells of a note found in Michelangelo's studio after he died. ... Scribbled by the elderly artist to an apprentice, it reads: "Draw, Antonio, draw, Antonio, draw and do not waste time."[24]

Jay Leno's brand of humor on *The Tonight Show* shows Americans how much they don't know about the past. Man-on-the-street-interviews asking low-level questions—for example, "Who was our nation's first president?" or "Who wrote the Ten Commandments?"—finds Jay giggling after hearing absurd answers to easy queries. Head-shaking aside, our collective historical amnesia may suggest a more serious dilemma. Can a family, nation, social group, or church have a future without a past? Is it possible to say why we exist without remembering why?

The 2008 Bradley Project on America's National Identity[25] should have sounded alarms across America's schoolrooms. The report maintains,

> Schools should ... begin with the study of America's great ideals, heroes, and achievements, so that its struggles can be put in perspective. A broad-minded, balanced approach to the American story best prepares young people for informed democratic participation ... The teaching of American history should be strengthened by including more compelling narratives and primary texts, such as the Declaration of Independence, the Constitution, and the great speeches and debates.[26]

The church, too, is at risk in every generation if it fails to teach its own history. The decline of mainline Protestantism can be seen in the microcosm of the Episcopal Church. Falls Church in Falls Church, Virginia seceded from denominational headquarters in the West, allying itself with the more conservative Nigerian Episcopalian conference on the African continent.[27] Why? In large measure, Episcopalian leadership in the West gives little foundation for its faith. Gone is a literal Genesis, a physical incarnation, or historical resurrection of Jesus from the dead.[28] Without documentation establishing past roots, little interest can be generated in future responsibility.

Alzheimer's disease robs one's mind of the past. However, neither this debilitating neurological condition, nor amnesia, nor a simple lapse defines the biblical basis for memory loss. The Hebrew word for "forget" tells us that overlooking God is an act of rebellion, an ethical choice to ignore.[29] Christians who remember, celebrate, and teach the past give renewed credence to the reliability, authenticity, and authority of history.

Three times in Deuteronomy 8:11–20, God's people were commanded not to ignore their Maker. Implied in the passage is the process of "forgetting God": apathy leads to pride, ultimately resulting in idolatry. "Being too full of oneself" begins the downward slide of disregarding the Almighty, which seems to take very little time.[30] Ezekiel 16:43–63 explains the outcomes of choosing to forget, one of which is the need to fear others.[31]

Everyone bows the knee to someone. James 1:25 explains that one antidote to forgetfulness is activity. The Sabbath is a sign practiced now through community celebration of Jesus' resurrection. Feasts, stones, tassels, table tops, and repositories for Scripture were the premise for active reminders through monuments, holidays, and medallions.[32] We make history live again by singing, pledging, bowing, eating, and drinking with gratefulness to God for who He is and what He has done.

Since people deliberately forget, we have to be reminded not to forget. So, the apostle Peter says, we must "recall the words," getting people to remember for themselves.[33] Vigen Guroian stresses the importance of teachers to ensure collective memory is passed on, renewed by each successive generation.[34] Explaining to classroom children why we have days off solidifies the reason for any season again and again. Community commitment to the past reminds us it's not about us, but it is up to us.

Perhaps the most vexing problem of indifference and ignorance of history is its basic state of ingratitude. Forgetting God and human agents of divine transformation in any country is a slap in the face to heaven and those on earth who have fostered freedoms we now take for granted. The teaching of history is a salute to the past and a stabilizing view toward the future. Remembering history is an active, collective, repetitive, and reflective process. Memory loss leads to lost motivation. The future is always dependent upon the past. "Knowledge can be lost. Sometimes this is perfectly reasonable: No one knows how to kill and skin a mastodon anymore, for obvious reasons. And ... you'd be hard pressed to find anyone who could write a computer program on punch-cards today. But there is something worrisome about misplacing knowledge that is only a generation or two old. And this happens more often than you might think."[35]

After my PhD graduation, mom gave me a gift, a labor of love, which is a pictorial history of photographs dating back to my great-grandmother. There will be many hours spent in gazing over the album, considering my past. Study must begin by preserving the past, for by it, we know better how to live, what to live for, and what is most important. Nations, churches, families, and individuals have no future if they forget to study their past.

Study: Student as Vocation

We must learn, then live.

Can a soldier be saved? Martin Luther wrote a booklet by that title. Luther argued God had appointed earthly rulers to restrain sin and given them the authority to "bear the sword." Gifted by God in this life, soldiers can know Scripture legitimizes their place. Luther said the soldier should think, "It is not I that slay, but God and my prince, for my hand and my body are now their servants." Humble and reserved before God, soldiers should "smite [the enemy] with a confident and untroubled spirit."[36] Shouldn't we be glad some have the calling to shoulder arms against evildoers? Aren't we pleased that our physical safety is helped by people dedicated to the task? All people, no matter who they are, what they do, or how old they are, have a calling.

Over more than twenty-five years teaching junior high through master's-level students, this idea that students have a calling has pressed on my mind. Views of vocation or "calling"[37] seem to be left for later in life, after schooling is complete. But I would contend that from the earliest period of their lives, young people can practice their vocation as students. Teachers must help students to see they should learn, then live.

When teens whine, "We have to go to school!" the suggestion becomes that academy work is an imposed tyranny. The proper attitude would be to accept the responsibility and fulfill the gifts of being students. The teaching of providence—God personally plans and oversees all events—suggests that our times, places, and opportunities are dependent upon heaven. With the command to scatter and multiply in Genesis 1 came the designation of people by language and territory. "I summon from a far-off land, a man to fulfill my purpose," God told His people. And Paul's apologetic for "the unknown God" includes the fact that He "determined the times set for [every nation] and the exact places where they should live."[38] For students to complain about their placement in human affairs is to question heaven.

Students are in the exact moment for which God has ordained their presence. Psalm 31:15 explains, "My times are in His hands." C. S. Lewis adds, "A man's upbringing, his talents, his circumstances, are usually a tolerable index of his vocation. If our parents have sent us to Oxford, if our country allows us to remain there, this is evidence that the life which we, at any rate, can best lead to the glory of God at present is the learned life."[39] The Christian teaching of providence in time tells the class we are to learn, then live.

The old adage "too soon old, too late smart" suggests youth has the power of strength yet great weakness in wisdom. Ecclesiastes says it best, "Be happy, young man, while you are young and let your heart give you joy in the days of your youth. Follow the ways of your heart and whatever your eyes see, but know that for all these things God will bring you to judgment ... Remember your Creator in the days of your youth" (11:9, 12:1). In our youth, there will be things we regret (not standing up for others), things we wish we would have continued (piano lessons), and things we've done we wish we had not. (The list is endless.) School days must be among those things for which Solomon encouraged full participation laden with great responsibility.

We must encourage high school students that this may be the last time they have time to study. Teenagers need to read big books, write big papers, and converse about big ideas. Why? Not only will everyone spend the rest of his or her life working, but each tick of the clock also brings us one second closer to death. Psalm 39:4–5 exclaims, "Show me, O Lord, my life's end and the number of my days; let me know how fleeting is my life ... each man's life is but a breath." Students must be impressed that preparation for the rest of life begins with our lives as students.

But some may ask, "How much time is necessary for life preparation?" The providence of time gives ample example. John Mark, in Paul's mind, needed over a dozen years to be helpful to the apostle's ministry.[40] And for his part, at least thirteen years preceded Paul's first missionary journey. Paul's pedigree was second to none, but he needed preparation for his new ministry.[41] After killing the Egyptian, God gave Moses forty years of leadership training prior to the Exodus.[42] And our Lord was thirty before His ministry began as recorded in the gospels. If time is important even in the human development of Jesus, how much more for students preparing for life?

The providence of time for students to grow in their thinking is buttressed by the teaching of place in God's economy. Genesis 10, Isaiah 46, and Acts 17 give evidence that where we live is important to the Creator. Students must learn to appreciate the places where they live that encourage learning. Many children throughout the world work to support their families from the earliest years. Teachers must point out the privilege of providence in allowing students to learn, then live. Often teenagers are anxious to get out or get away from hometowns without understanding what they have or what they give up. "All the days ordained for me were written in your book" (Psalm 139:16) encourages gratitude for a student's time and place. Instructing now for the acquisition of knowledge that will be lived later is the Christian premise of study.

The comment most rehearsed from students over my years of teaching is, "I wish I had paid better attention in class." Yet some are anxious to learn. The teaching of providence in opportunity is summarized well by James 4:13–17. "What is your life? You are a mist that appears for a little while and then vanishes … you ought to say, 'If it is the Lord's will, we will live and do this or that.'" Everyone lives at the behest of the Sovereign of the universe. What is a student's responsibility? Ephesians 5:16 answers, "To buy up every opportunity." Students should thank God for their providential opportunity to learn in this place and time.

In eighth grade, I couldn't wait to go to high school. In high school, I anticipated college. Collegiate experience prompted dreams of grad school. You know what I learned? Don't wish for time to go faster. The clock seems to race against itself. Applications to life today abound. Time allows for opportunity; don't waste it. Place is community; don't take it for granted. Gratitude is a mark of character; give it. Students must thank parents, administration, teachers, and of course, their Creator for student life afforded them now.

We are personally indebted to soldiers who execute their calling with vigor. Indeed, I revel in the business of every person's gifts. Vocation is not something that will happen later in life. Calling in the earliest years of life is to be a student. Preparation must precede ministry. Study must come before work. Learning must set the stage for living.

Study: The Art of War

Victory loves preparation.

Studying the art of war is crucial for preparation to fight in war. Retired Major General Robert H. Scales argues that a national defense is dependent upon soldiers' ability to think critically. After making his case, Scales concludes, "War is a thinking man's game and only those who take the time to study war are likely to fight it competently. Soldiers and Marines need time for reflection, time to learn, teach, research and write."[43] Every vocation necessitates education built on knowledge. Students of every stripe must learn, then live.

"School" came from the Latin *schole*, meaning "leisure." The idea was that such a prolonged opportunity for focused study would never come again. Billy Graham was asked what he would do differently if he had life to live over again. His response, without hesitation, was that he would study twice as much as he ministered. John Wesley, given a hypothetical situation of knowing he had three years to live, was questioned how he would use the time. His reply was to the point: "I would study for two and preach for one." Every builder, athlete, businessperson, restaurateur—*everyone*—knows action without plan is a mitigated disaster. Planning is based on knowing.

"It is not good to have zeal without knowledge, or be hasty and miss the way."[44] Hebrew readers understood that *zeal* meant excitement without direction. They would not make snap judgments, as one who was *hasty*. Like the carpenter, people were taught to measure twice and cut once. They would gain understanding little by little, supported by the wisdom of Proverbs 21:5: "The plans of the diligent lead to profit as surely as haste leads to poverty." Not *missing the way*, listeners were to keep their eyes on the prize. Unlike the fool whose eyes "wandered to the ends of the earth" without focus, "a discerning man kept wisdom in view."[45]

Learning and then living takes concerted effort. Learning is work. Work was commissioned by God as good before human sin.[46] But ever since Genesis 3, the task of learning demands we overcome the weeds of study. When students whine, "Why do we have to take the test?" the requisite answer is, "Because you're sinners!" Frustration arises out of learning, because learning takes a long time. Someone once asked me in the midst of an interim pulpit supply how long a certain sermon had taken to develop. My answer of three years prompted wide-eyed shock! But such is the case. If learning is work, my fallen, fragile mind demands long-term dedication.

For the Christian, then, an intentional steadfastness to learning precedes all else. A second major principle for a student's vocation is the discipleship of the mind to scholarship. Solomon's response to the Almighty's offer of any gift in 1 Kings 3:7–9 was an earnest desire for wisdom, knowledge, and understanding. Scripture takes up mentoring the mind throughout its pages. Romans 8:6–8 mandates the Christian mind be Spirit-controlled. Believers see the world through the lens of the Word. A process of renewal develops through the transformation begun in the mind, explains Romans 12:2. Changed thinking is the result of sanctified thinking. Every Christian should pray with the Psalmist in 119:18, "Open my eyes that I might see wonderful things in your law." Precepts from Holy Writ are available to students strapped into the harness of a Spirit-directed, disciplined mind. Only then can the believer hope to fulfill the command of 2 Corinthians 10:5: "Bring every thought captive to Christ."

But doesn't our culture worship at the altar of education? Must we not be careful that intellectual pursuits do not derail us from spiritual maturity in Christ? Some fall prey to the academy's manipulations. Worshipping the intellect over the Creator is problematic if that is our focus.[47] In similar fashion, arrogance producing a big head is not to be a Christian response to knowledge.[48] But perhaps the spirit of any human-centered age is best represented in Paul's warning that some are "ever learning but never coming to the truth."[49] Discipleship of the Christian mind runs counter to all these distortions, as we have the mind of Christ.[50]

Having the mind of Christ is one thing; changing our minds toward a proper view of learning is something else. In all my years of teaching, I have *never* heard anyone say we do our homework to the glory of God. If mediocrity is unacceptable on an athletic field, shouldn't this also be true of the classroom? Students should learn to give God glory. Psalm 115:1 is clear;

our lives are to give God's name glory. Life is God-given. This God-given life is sacred. Sacred, God-given life brings responsibility. And responsibility to sacred, God-given life is lifelong.[51] As students, we give ourselves to knowledge, because the knowledge has been given to us.

What applications arise from a God-centered view of knowledge? Why should we learn, then live?

1. We should understand there is always more to learn, remaining teachable.[52]
2. We should commit ourselves with discipline to every discipline.[53]
3. Success in education is not high test scores but faithfulness to the duties of discernment.[54]
4. Stewardship of knowledge necessitates that we dedicate ourselves to our studies.[55]
5. School exercises—each being fragments of eternal truth—are like sacraments to God.[56]
6. Security of truth rests with us.[57]

As C. S. Lewis said,

> If all the world were Christian, it might not matter if all the world were uneducated. But as it is, a cultural life will exist outside the Church whether it exists inside or not. To be ignorant and simple now—not to be able to meet the enemies on their own ground—would be to throw down our weapons, and to betray our uneducated brethren who have, under God, no defense but us against the intellectual attacks of the heathen. Good philosophy must exist, if for no other reason, because bad philosophy needs to be answered.[58]

I once asked a student what her school was known for. Her academy, by her account, was seen as a party school. Who is responsible for such a situation? Who should carry out the applications student as a vocation? Vigilance to carry out the mission of the school falls to administration. To stop mission drift, headmasters must anchor their thinking in a vocational commitment to biblical thought. Teachers form the second line of defense.

A view of life is intentionally taught in every lesson, reinforced in every activity, and revisited at every relational opportunity. Students themselves bear responsibility to remember what was said at the outset: preparation precedes activity, knowing establishes doing, and principle frames practice. Warriors study war. Christians, as students, must study the Word to prepare for the world.

Retreat: Cutting Wood on Sunday

Rest is doing something other than what we normally do.

When I was a high school teacher, I loved cutting wood on Sunday. Chainsaws, wedges, mauls, axes, and muscle were all employed with gusto to create brush burn piles or stack cordwood. My sedentary work as an educator necessitated I do something else for rest after remembrance at my local church's worship service. Growing up in an assembly controlled by legalism, I had to grow out of the mind-set that mowing grass or any other physical labor on Sunday was a sin.

On the other side of the globe, the Japanese are known for being an industrious people. In the 1980s, the land of the rising sun set worldwide industry standards for work. But something else came out of Japan. The island nation has a word for extreme commitment to labor: *karoshi,* meaning "death by overwork." But patterns of overwork are not relegated to one people group. Eugene Peterson says it best:

> Most of us spend most of our time in the workplace. But without Sabbath ... the workplace is soon emptied of any sense of the presence of God and the work becomes an end in itself. It is this "end in itself" that makes an un-sabbathed workplace a breeding ground for idols. We make idols in our workplaces when we reduce all relationship to functions that we can manage. We make idols in our work places when we reduce work to the dimensions of our egos and control.
>
> When we work we are most god-like, which means that it is in our work that it is easiest to develop god-pretensions.

Un-sabbathed, our work becomes the entire context in which we define our lives. We lose God-consciousness, God-awareness, sightings of resurrection. We lose the capacity to sing "This is my Father's world" and end our chirping little self-centered ditties about what *we* are doing and feeling.[59]

Leviticus 23:1–3 instructs the reader, "Six days you may work," indicating a creation pattern. The Genesis command to manage and conserve creation, the fruit of one's labor, is *not* to become the end-all of life. "You are not to do any work" is a release, *not* a restriction for our profit. The Creator has our best interests at heart.[60] "The seventh day is a Sabbath of rest" reads "rest, rest" in the Hebrew and is a literary devise for emphasis. Production *increases* when people are rested; reaping requires rest.

What kind of work was Yahweh restricting or banning on the Sabbath? The original word used almost exclusively in the Sabbath-rest-holiday discussion[61] is the term that means our vocational, God-given abilities.[62] God ceased His creative creating as Creator. Jesus—God in flesh on earth—even rested from His ministry functions in Mark 6:30–32.

Israel was an agricultural culture. Its need of rest was to cease from practicing planting, sowing, reaping, or any physical labor related to its people's six-day routines. The application is clear: we need to rest from our giftedness. Here are five questions we should ask ourselves:

1. What is my vocation, calling, business—my normal work?
2. Do my Sabbaths include remembrance and rest?
3. Do I recall why my Sabbath is important?
4. Do I spend my Sabbath pouring myself into something else?
5. Do I allow my vocation, my work, to run my life?

God established retreat as Genesis law. The third pre-fall blessing from God was *creational*, embedded as necessary in God's world. I learned from a farmer friend in South Dakota that his work tending the soil ended for one twenty-four-hour period each week. Larry's *individual* commitment to Sabbath was based on his weekly work obligations. The only one of the Ten Commandments not repeated in the Second Testament means that no one should tell another when to practice rest.[63] A *liberal* (or broadminded) approach to retreat must be based on liberty, not legislation.[64] Respecting the convictions of others is important in the church. An individual's decision to rest arises out of *vocational* concerns. God-gifted business, education, homemaking, construction, or industry workers will direct people's retreats in different ways.

A number of years ago, I wrote a poem to remind myself that retreat is crucial:

Lord, when the alarm clock, stove clock, and time clock demand my presence,
When the pace of life is hectic,
When I wish there were six more hours in a day,
When the traffic light is stuck on red
And my family's schedule demands I be in three places at one time,
May I take time to rest, Lord.

Lord, when people expect too much of me,
When the boss has forgotten about the eight-hour day,
When I am constantly at others' beck and call,
When the cell phone, Twitter, fax, and email all go off at once
And I begin to hate the human race,
May I take time to rest, Lord.

Lord, when work occupies all my waking hours,
When television commercials say I must have more,
When my neighbors flaunt their newest toys,
When alcoholic does not apply but workaholic does
And I decide to go to the office on Sunday to catch up,
May I take time to rest, Lord.

Lord, when money means more than people,
When I read *The Wall Street Journal* more than my Bible,
When overtime becomes my primetime,
When promotions and pay hikes are my ultimate goals
And looking out for number one has become my slogan in life,
May I take time to rest, Lord.

Lord, may I refocus my life on you.

May I restore my thoughts in your Word.

May I refresh my schedule by meditating on all your blessings.

May I relax my activity every week to enjoy the life you gave me.

May I take time to rest, Lord.

Retreat: It Is Finished

Celebration is a good reason to rest.

When I finish mowing the lawn, cleaning the house, or eating leftovers, I step back to view a job well done.[65] When God finished creation, He celebrated—twice—the meaning of the word "rest" in Genesis 2:3.[66] Humans are imprinted with our Creator's image to work and then relish our labor's results.

"It is finished,"[67] Genesis 2:1–2 adds. The Sabbath begins by ending. The Hebrew word demands we quit! Stop! Break the routine! Order is given to the week by ceasing our labor. Significance to the first six days is given importance by the seventh—there is a freedom from production and acquisition. Genesis 1:31 declares enjoyment in what has been made by contemplating the beauty in the enterprise (2:9). Exodus 31:17 repeats the process of creation for refreshment ("to take a breath") by taking delight in what is witnessed.

Let's dispel the wrong notion: God did not rest because He was tired after work. Instead, God set a precedent, establishing a life principle. Hawaiians say *pau*—God stopped because He was finished, not fatigued. Five times in three verses, "the seventh day" appears. Sabbath sets a rhythm, pattern, refrain, or cadence,[68] giving significance to every other day for creation to operate in a certain way.

Once God completed His task, there is a repetition-escalation in the text; it looks like this in Hebrew: "God finished the work[69] He had done from all the work He had done from all the creation work He had done" (Genesis 2:2–3). These phrases, building on each other, explain what "God finished" means. First, there is no longer a physical creation going on. Second, rest is the end of creation, an anticipation of something yet to come. Third, there is a marker of the world to come—namely, eternity is the goal; people are made for eternity. Notice that the normal end phrase to the first six days is not repeated here; the "evening and morning" formula is absent. If eternity is the goal, evening and morning are unnecessary. Hebrews 4:9–10 summarizes: rest is God's original intention. Rest is the eternal anticipation of His people.

In 1987, I preached my first sermon on Sabbath[70]. I wrote a rudimentary poem to remind myself of what rest means for everyone:

> God gave a special day,
> Because all people are made of clay
> So that believers could pray
> And all people could play.

"Worry. Don't be happy!" rightly explodes the myth that happiness is our highest human goal.[71] Another wrong view from ancient times believed leisure was for the wealthy and ruling classes, never for anyone else. There are no parallels from Near Eastern cultures for a day of rest-celebration. In fact, the Greeks thought the Jews were lazy for taking the day off! On the contrary, Isaiah 58:9 declares that delight should be a byproduct of celebrating a *holiday*—a seventh, set-apart day. Ecclesiastes, my favorite Bible book, sings the chorus of Sabbath enjoyment: life is a gift of God, so enjoy it![72]

Jesus reemphasized the significance of Sabbath by infusing Sabbath rest *into* people. Mark 2:23–28 and 3:1–6 establish Jesus' point of view. The Sabbath is made for humanity; it is beneficial. The Sabbath is for restoration—a pointer to perfection in eternity. The Sabbath is for peace; the Man of Sorrows takes our sorrows. But in Matthew 11:28, Sabbath bursts into daily living: "Come to me and I will rest (Sabbath) you, you will find rest (Sabbath) for your souls." Augustine's famous line is no better understood than here: "You have made us for yourself and our hearts find no rest until the rest in you." It is the person of Jesus who sanctified the seventh day in Genesis and declared us holy-rested through His sanctification.

When I finish this essay, I will read it again any number of times. I find delight in the placement of words, creation of sentences, construction of paragraphs, and building of essays. Normally, people return again and again to museums, marveling at the works of art. All of us return to our work, in one way or another, to witness a job well done. Why not? We image God's image, work His works, and celebrate His celebration.

Retreat: Naked in the Universe

Sabbath forces us to look up to the One who
has given us Genesis law down here.

Friends shower me with birthday greetings on Facebook each year. Students from my past school years send additional messages— things they recollected from my instruction. A few that stand out are the remembrances of my antipathy for the word *vacation*. "You are *not* to go on vacation! These days off from school are a *holiday!* Don't forget the Americans who died (Memorial Day), sacrificed (Veteran's Day), served (President's Day), worked (Labor Day), started (Thanksgiving), and motivated (Martin Luther King Jr. Day) our country!" Included in my harangue would be a plea to remember Sabbath—to recall why we work and who gave us the privilege.

The fourth commandment is the longest of all and the only one of the ten *not* repeated in the Second Testament.[73] It is a positive command—a release from, not subservient to time. For those who would denigrate the First Testament as arcane, an awful imposition on people, God's Word was a halogen headlight in the darkness of the ancient Near Eastern world. Unlike any other nation, Israel treated people as people, not property. Outsiders and strangers were incorporated in the weekly celebration. Even animals were included.[74] Leviticus 23:1–3 sets precedent and principle for keeping the Sabbath for both remembrance and rest.

Israel held a weekly convention.[75] Sabbath was for commemoration.[76] Holidays had a purpose. Holidays created memories, reminded people of their place, established repetition, formed memorials, and produced anticipation.[77] Scripture heralds further ideas not already mentioned: Sabbath was a sign between God and His people; blessing resulted from keeping the day; treating Sabbath like any other day was grounds for chastisement;

Sabbath was made for people; and external appearances were no way to judge a person's activities on the Sabbath.[78] Sabbath was to be a collective event; there were no geographical boundaries.[79] Sabbath was a contemplative focus on Yahweh.[80]

But like every other gift given for our benefit, we humans mess it up. Sin always produces extremes. In the First Testament, folks just plain did not keep the Sabbath. One of the reasons for a seventy-year exile in Babylon was that the land rest law was not practiced. Second Chronicles 36:21 records God's specific reason given for national discipline: for at least 490 years, fields were not rested, and soil nutrients were not replenished. Gardening is the first work of the Almighty in His creation. Land and place are of primary importance in His decrees for Israel. So it should come as no surprise that the reason why beans, tomatoes, corn, and other crops should be rotated in a garden is for the sake of the soil.

The pendulum then swung the other way. Exile sharpened Israel's focus on God. Yet over time, law became legalism, and regulation replaced rest. Pharisees debated the definition of work. For example, should one walk one or two miles on Sabbath? Loopholes were created. One group said that a person could travel one mile before Sabbath, find a tree, and deposit food there, declaring the spot temporary housing. When the last day of the week began a few moments later, the individual could then walk another mile![81]

Blaise Pascal, the brilliant seventeenth-century Christian mathematician, zeroes in on the necessity of both/and instead of either/or. In his *Pensees* (or *Thoughts*), Pascal records two statements, one after the other, explaining our two problems—the two sides of the same sinful coin. *Restlessness* is a result of the laborer who works too hard. *Weariness* is the result of a man with nothing to do. Nothing is so insufferable to man as to be completely at rest, without passions, business, diversion, or study. He then feels his nothingness, forlornness, insufficiency, dependence, weakness, and emptiness. There will immediately arise from the depth of his heart weariness, gloom, sadness, fretfulness, vexation, and despair.[82]

Interestingly, Pascal refers to the overworked as *restless* and the one who has no work as *weary*. I have spent some time displaced from vocational service. Focus, meaning, and purpose were taken from me. Pascal's words are exact replicas of my experience. Yet when I was fully employed with much on my plate, I found my mind wandering, looking, anticipating something else. The results of no rest or too much rest in Israel's day are no different than in our own: the gift is either misused or not used at all. "[Work] saves man from the solitariness that he fears ... for when a man is alone he is really alone ... he is then naked in the universe; he is face to face with God; and this confrontation is formidable ... Modern man ... takes refuge in anesthetics, and most of all the opiate of work, which keeps his thoughts away from contemplation by keeping his eyes fixed on the conveyor belt or the drawing board."[83]

Sabbath compels us to be alone with God. Perhaps this is why we replace remembrance of God's gift with more work or more rules. Perhaps we do not use the word *holiday* because of its meaning: a day set apart or holy. *Vacation* comes from the Latin root "to vacate," "leave empty," or in our parlance, veg out! It may be easier for us to erase responsibility for the Sabbath than to remember it. Memorials are forgotten both to our shame and loss. Sabbath forces us to look up to the One who has given us Genesis law down here.

Retreat: Pig Roast

Time can be saved.

O nce upon a time in China, a family left their home to visit the next village. While they were gone, embers from a cooking stove caught the house on fire, burning it to the ground. Returning to the same day's destruction, the father found the pet pig roasted within the structure. Not wishing to waste any food, the animal was carved into multiple meals. From that time on, whenever someone wanted to have pork barbeque, he burned down his home. The Chinese moral to the story is clear: *do not sacrifice what is important on the altar of insignificance.*

Genesis establishes significance for humanity. The first five Bible books were written by Moses after the exodus from Egypt. In order to establish a written history of God's world, Genesis is written as an apologetic, a defense of the Hebrew worldview. Genesis takes a stand against the polytheistic worlds of Egypt and then Canaan, the land God's chosen were about to enter. The first eleven chapters of Scripture are a statement declaring the distinction between the personal, eternal, triune Creator and unreal pagan idols. In the pagan mind-set, creation gives order; in Israel's thinking, God orders creation.

On the first parchment page of God's revelation to humanity, the declaration is clear: worship the One who creates creation. People of the day had seven-day cycles, as did Israel. However, the days were tied to moon phases and considered to be bad luck. Avoidance of pleasure or projects was important to discourage evil omens.[84] Completely different, Israel was not tied to heavenly cycles but to heaven. A day of refreshment and renewal mimicked the Creator.

Genesis is in agreement with our daily lives. The world works in a certain way; we know we need rest. A creational ordinance or what I call Genesis law means that God established regularity and pattern within His world. For instance, on average, humans spend one-third of their lives asleep. Biologists tell us that prior to mitosis, the matter within the cell interfaces or rests in anticipation of dividing itself. Many more examples could follow: sun and rain, seasonal changes, and the day-night cycle. Clearly, rest is embedded within creation itself.

The creational ordinance of rest is a distinctive blessing given by the personal Creator in the opening pages of His book. God gave three blessings prior to human sin: *reproduction* (Genesis 1:22), *rule* (1:28), and *rest* (2:3). The word used for *rest* literally means to cease from one's work for a time.[85] Once begun, the pattern should continue. The importance of *rest* as a blessing cannot be overemphasized. In ancient Near Eastern religions, people created holy places, holy men, and holy things. But for Israel, the first thing God made holy was a time for rest.

Egypt, Canaan, and all the nations of Israel's day sanctified space, a place, a piece of creation. God's first use of the word *holy*—distinctiveness, a set-apart nature—is to sanctify time.[86] The first instance of the word *holy* in Scripture stipulates that God wants His people to be different by making time holy.[87] The climax of creation is to construct one day out of seven as unique. *Holi*day—a day set apart—should mark our calendars rather than vacation, coming from the Latin meaning to evacuate or leave empty. When time is sanctified, our days are given meaning.

Ephesians 5:16 commands us to redeem the time by buying it back, making the most of every opportunity, giving time purpose. Second Corinthians 6:2 admonishes humans not to take time for granted, because "today is the day of salvation": tomorrow has no guarantee. Psalm 31:15 makes the Lord lord of tomorrow, saying, "My times are in His hand." "Don't boast about tomorrow, for you don't know what a day may bring," Proverbs 27:1 reminds us. James 4:14 calls life "a vapor." Psalm 90:9–12 reminds everyone that time is short, so people should calculate, take stock of, or number their days. Every tick of the clock brings us one second closer to death—far from morbid, the statement forbids nonchalance in life.

Time is precious. I rue the days when I was five that I did not take advantage of naptime—I wish I could take those naps now! My constant harangue to teenagers who cannot wait to get out of high school goes something like this: "For most of you, this is probably the last time someone else will pay to put a roof over your head and food in your stomach! Don't wish for time to go faster! Time goes fast enough!" We must not waste time. Time should not be killed (as in, "I'm just killing time"). Time is not money: time cannot be commercialized if it is a gift. Our culture places dollar signs on the clock. Unbelieving mind-sets today are the same as those of the ancients. We worship creation instead of the Creator. We worship time instead of the timekeeper.

The clock reminds every athletic contestant as it does every human that there is only so much time to play the game. As in sports, so in life, we answer to an authority outside of ourselves. To worship the Creator is to remember He made an ordered universe for our benefit. A return to Genesis law in our thinking is to acknowledge His beneficence and practice the blessing of *shabbat,* Sabbath, rest, retreat. The three blessings of Genesis 1:22, 28 and 2:3 are all commands: the first two are given directly, and the third is only reported, its enactment altogether beyond human control.[88]

Retreat is not a luxury. Retreat is an expectation, an act of worship, and the anticipation of eternity.[89] Retreat is not something we work into our schedules; our schedules should work around retreat. To think that we can honor the Creator by carving out time for retreat is burning the house to barbeque a pig. We must not offer what is important on the altar of insignificance.

Retreat: The Slowness of God

God's Word begins and ends with rest.

"Genesis is a myth, a story of origins like other stories," began the college professor. During my tenure as a Christian school teacher, I had my students compare Genesis 1–3 with nonhistorical explanations of earth's origins. After completing a paper pointing out the similarities and differences between Genesis and fictional accounts of our beginnings, I asked a local professor to teach my students his point of view: Genesis is no different than comparable fables.

Joseph Campbell, encouraged by journalists like Bill Moyers, fostered the fraud of Genesis equality with ancient fabrications for the '80s generation. Impact from false teaching about Genesis' historicity has devastated the church. Born of poor doctrinal church instruction, college students are turned from biblical truth by college educators questioning the first pages of Scripture. More and more so-called "evangelicals" have subscribed to the current craze that Adam and Eve are not historical. Popular novels such as Dan Brown's *The Da Vinci Code* have cemented cultural confusion that God's Word is historically unreliable.

Stripping Genesis of its one-of-a-kind authenticity knocks out the foundation of true claims for every arena of life. The twin lies of consumerism and statism (the idea that government can solve our problems) are born of Genesis rejection. Earth-rape and earth-worship are sins against the personal Creator. Both individual perception and personal interpretation short-circuit Genesis law in literature, the arts, judicial oversight, and human relations. The lords of career and pleasure start from opposite ends of the spectrum: the idea that the only origins that matter are my own.

Like other sins, allowing work to dominate life without rest or rest to eliminate work is to strike a match to Genesis 1–2. Israel's neighbors believed humans were created to do the gods' work. Some cultural teaching—residue from the industrial revolution—created a servile class to meet the needs of industry owners. Others who believe there is no one or nothing above us make work their end-all. Wrong views of work and rest feed off each other. Pleasure-seeking, thank-goodness-it's-Friday, live-for-the-weekend views dominate materially wealthy countries. Forced laborers without adequate protection from any authority, bodies bent with pain, grind out their existence with little or no rest.

The so-called Protestant work ethic is either praised or vilified for its product. Those who denigrate Puritan resolve for hard work bypass both work's benefit and the appropriate stoppage of labor for adequate renewal. Yet Leland Ryken contends that the Puritans failed to give us a cohesive, heaven-sent story of rest simply because they tried to make leisure useful.[90] But Israel's Exodus narrative celebrated freedom from work.[91] Jewish scholar Abraham Heschel says the Sabbath celebration is "not a date but an atmosphere ... a taste of eternity—the world to come."[92]

Rest is both the beginning and end of the storybook. The pinnacle event of creation is Sabbath. Jesus, being Lord of the Sabbath, will return the world to its original intention. Egyptian, Babylonian, Assyrian, Canaanite, Persian, Greek, Roman, English, French, German, and American stories all end. And herein is the most basic difference between other cultures' nonhistorical myths and Genesis—"But when the fullness of time had come, God sent His Son ... He was foreknown before the foundation of the world but was made manifest in the last times for your sake ... I am the Alpha and the Omega, the first and the last, the beginning and the end."[93]

God acted in the exact, opportune moment. God's plan in time was set in eternity. God started what He will finish. God takes His time. God's work is slow. God is not bound to our timetables. God's snaillike pace is set against our day-timers, calendars, appointments, schedules, and routines. God's story is His story, not history. God's culmination of His intention at creation will end with rest. But "cleverly devised myths ... will say 'Where is the promise of His coming? For ever since the fathers fell asleep, all things are continuing as they were from the beginning of creation.'"[94]

Ancient and modern mythologies see time as a gerbil on the wheel, going round and round. Time has no end, so culture tells us to live for the moment. We work so we can rest, and our rest motivates our work. The problem with human myths is that they focus on us. The slowness of God in human events is born of Genesis 2 Sabbath. "But do not overlook this one fact, beloved, that with the Lord one day is as a thousand years, and a thousand years as one day. The Lord is not slow to fulfill His promise as some count slowness, but is patient toward you … But according to His promise we are waiting for new heavens and a new earth.[95]

"Are there any questions?" The professor's query was wrapped in a smug, pompous tone. What did these high school students know of Genesis and mythology? The arrogant attitude was immediately met with forty raised hands. His face registered a look of befuddlement. By the end of the question-and-answer, the self-important college elite stormed out of his own classroom, unable to answer my students' incisive questions. To this day, the full retelling of the event sends shivers down my spine. Eighteen-year-olds had correlated the ancient writings and found that only one told the whole, true story. Other stories are fabrications. The story—beginning and ending with rest—is the fabric of the world.

Discipline: Bathroom Scales

Wonder should cause us to wonder.

French women do not have scales in their bathrooms or get fat.[96] Mireille Guiliano suggests recasting as the way to curtail calorie counts. As most health professionals know, weight loss is not achieved through dieting but through proper diet and exercise.[97] Yet Americans spend over $50 billion on weight loss products, equal to the gross national product of Ireland.[98] Not included in this number is the amount that Americans spend each year on health clubs and gyms, a staggering $18.5 billion in 2007.[99] In the West, can we discipline ourselves through external controls?

In the East, internal compulsion is key. Yoga, for instance, is a practice that enhances physical activity with the union (the definition of "yoga") of spiritual wellbeing. Inner harmony, internal peace, and happiness are thought to be achieved through focus on one's inner self. Meditation seeks to empty people of everything to attain serenity. Focused on becoming their real selves, people are encouraged to discipline their lives to what Eckart Tolle calls *The Power of Now*.[100] But can individuals monitor themselves?

Governmental discipline is always in question. Across the country in 2010, concerned citizens organized tea parties to register their complaints against government taxation. At the same time, politicians used high executive salaries as a front, deflecting blame for personal lack of governmental oversight. Representatives in both houses of Congress allowed unhealthy fiscal practices for campaign revenue. But does regulation of an industry by those who profit from it create proper supervision?

Academics attempt to ensure accurate supervision through a practice called tenure. After a number of years, publications, and performance reviews, faculty members seek long-term connection to an institution. Juried or peer-reviewed journal articles are another attempt by the academy to give parameters to research. Dissertation committees make a student accountable to the directives of higher education. But do objective standards of conduct driven by subjective professors guarantee good teachers?

Discipline in all the spheres of life is impacted because of rootlessness. We have lost our center. Untethered, we float, weightless, lost in the cosmos. Gone is stability in what Francis Schaeffer called "true Truth."[101] Transcendence—the outside source of truth—is missing. G. K. Chesterton argued in *Orthodoxy* that Christian theology is "the best root of energy and sound ethics."[102] Henry Zylstra, in an essay entitled "Thoughts for Teachers," trains his crosshairs on the target: "We have to get squared around towards God if the universe is to make sense. Life is bewildering and meaningless without the fixed reference point. And how were one to find his way in a life of eternity with a map of time except he have a polar point, a Bethlehem, an Incarnation? Orientation: that is our work as teachers. We must give our pupils their bearings in life by causing them to face towards the east."[103]

Christian doctrine[104] or theology[105] is necessary to refocus on the cosmic center: Christ. In fact, one was thought to be healthy or well with the proper doctrine.[106] All other belief systems are dependent upon works for eternal life. Both Western and Eastern views of living leave one empty inside or out. Governmental and academic regulations relying on fallen, subjective people cannot produce an objective standard of reality. But Christian doctrine teaches that the gospel is wholly of grace, from God, making a person well from the inside out.[107]

Internal discipline was necessary to complete my PhD. My first response, when I returned to my room after my dissertation defense, was to weep. Yes, I was very tired. But there was a sense that not only had a great weight been lifted, but also that a great weight of responsibility had taken its place. Knowledge carries with it the essence of humility. It is true for me every time I study, read, write, think, or teach: I feel a deep wonder, an inexplicable honor to learn. To me, wonder is the doctrine necessary for discipline. At the end of my dissertation defense, I offered this assessment to my reviewers: "By The Spirit's work within me, I am grateful for this life and the opportunities of it. I give thanks to Him who has made me for His created world. I am satisfied with everything He has given to enjoy. I am humbled by how much there is to know and how little I know of it. And while He has crowned me with honor, all glory is due Him for His works and His work in me."[108]

Discipline necessitates Christian wonder. We do not need bathroom scales. We need to remove the scales from our eyes.

Discipline: What Kramer Asked George

Learning should be our yearning.

"Everything relates to *Seinfeld*." A running joke in our household and among friends for years, the '90s sitcom addresses many human concerns. In one episode entitled "The Keys,"[109] Kramer is disgusted with George, saying, "You're wasting your life!" George—ever paranoid, ever defensive—gives one pathetic response after another to Kramer's harangue that he has no reason to get up in the morning.[110] Later, as Kramer considers his own purpose for being, he asks George, "Do you *yearn?*"

George, unable to fathom the concept, replies with hesitation, "Well, not recently." A moment's pause prompts a final, feeble attempt to define *yearning:* "But I crave."

In a culture obsessed with the physical, craving has replaced yearning. As a high school teacher for seventeen years, it was my wish to create in students a yearning to learn. Yet how many times did I hear the infamous, "How will I use *this?*" Plagued by consumerism, we in the West have misused the practical, creating pragmatism. No longer content to pursue a coherent framework of knowledge, degrees are instead keys, unlocking more fiscal rewards. Unfortunately, like George, the idea of desire is reduced to lust. Harry R. Lewis, former dean of Harvard College, lamented the educational state of affairs as *Excellence Without a Soul.*[111]

Hebrews set the standard, using the word for "soul" as equivalent to yearning. "My soul yearns for you in the night; in the morning my spirit longs for you."[112] The soul can be hungry or thirsty.[113] Some satisfy satisfaction with appetite, craving what they lack.[114] Ecclesiastes says folks fill the void with more emptiness, others "with good things."[115] "As the deer pants for streams of water, so my soul pants for you, O God."[116] Loving God with the whole of one's life ("heart, soul, strength," according to Deuteronomy 6:5) is singular devotion, one's desire. But what is it that prompts our longing to love God?

Jonathan Edwards in a sermon entitled "The Importance and Advantage of a Thorough Knowledge of Divine Truth"[117] explains,

> So there can be no love without knowledge. It is not according to the nature of the human soul, to love an object which is entirely unknown. The heart cannot be set upon an object of which there is no idea in the understanding. The reasons which induce the soul to love, must first be understood, before they can have a reasonable influence on the heart. God hath given us the Bible ... there can be no spiritual knowledge of that of which there is not first a rational knowledge.

Solomon was right: "It is not good to have zeal (Hebrew "soul") without knowledge."[118] It seems that yearning, a longing for God, one's desire "indeed is the desire to know, for we are known, and into this we grow."[119] Eugene Peterson calls knowing God *ascetical theology*. "No wonder there is such lavish attention given throughout Scripture to the properties and conditions of our humanity—our bodily parts, our emotional states, our physical circumstances, our mental processes, our geographical settings. Every human detail is part of this instrumentality of response to God."[120]

My daughter, Chelsea, after completing her undergraduate degree, told me she had now learned how to be a student. She is in exactly the right frame of mind to live a whole Christian life. Edwards contends that knowing about God and His world is the "daily business" of all Christians, "their high calling," benefiting the soul.[121] "Hard work and discipline should be needed for this," maintains Evelyn Underhill. In a chapter entitled "The Preparation of a Mystic," she contends that knowledge development will entail "the training of a layer of your consciousness which has lain fallow in the past."[122] The so-called spiritual disciplines need biblical knowledge to prompt desire for loving God in everything.

I was with a group of church elders at a retreat center. Anxious to learn, they asked, "If we set up a group, can we study Scripture together?" Unlike George, here are believers that know yearning is a desire for our Father, knowing His Son, attained through the Spirit's discipline by reading the book.

Discipline: "I Love Those Guys"

We are joined together in a battle for ideas.

"They saved my life ... These are great men; they are heroes." During a forty-five-minute fire-fight with Islamic terrorists, an embedded journalist was pulled out of harm's way by American soldiers who placed the importance of another's life above their own.

"I love those guys," David Beriain said, looking wistfully out the window ... "From the first time you go kick a door with them, they accept you—you're one of them. I've even got a 'family photo' with them ... It is those common experiences, where you are all in danger, and you go through it together. It builds a relationship instantly."[123]

Whatever one's view of war, objective observers recognize the importance of kinship in combat. A soldier fights for his or her country and the soldier next to him or her.

Neither can the battle for ideas be fought alone. A quote from Charles Haddon Spurgeon has hung in my office for years: "The man who never reads will never be read; he who never quotes will never be quoted. He who will not use the thoughts of other men's brains, proves that he has no brains of his own."[124] Spurgeon would have appreciated the latest development in Bible study: the InterVarsity Press series *Ancient Christian Commentary on Scripture*.[125] The voices of church fathers are being heard again. Thousands of books like these line shelves in my library, the collected wisdom of giants on whose shoulders I stand.

It was with great sadness, then, that I read some believe humanity's curricula around the United States will have to justify its existence.[126] However, almost four hundred reactions to the article's negative slant on the liberal arts give hope. Most of the respondents expressed similar ideas: learning the great works of others had disciplined them into thinking people.

In "Why Should Businessmen Read Great Literature?" Vigen Guroian argues that ethics are best learned not from textbooks, but from Shakespeare and Dostoevsky. "To be free, [means] to grow into fuller, more complete, and more interesting human beings who share with each other a living and a life-giving culture."[127] We should read great books. Wise voices from the past can help develop the discipline of community ideas today.

Great people read great books. President George W. Bush read voluminously during his presidency. Over the last three years of his tenure, our forty-third president read almost two hundred books. In addition, he read the Bible cover-to-cover each year.[128] History and biography are prominent in the president's reading list. Learning from others in history influences the discipline of how we live together now.

Community reading prompted Kenneth Badley to write an article that encourages concerned church members to read along with college undergraduates:

> Students live in a vulnerable position. They must face the challenges of the world of thought while assuming no conflict exists between the truth therein and the truth of Scripture. Presumably they do so with God's help, but, as I have described it, they will do so without any supporting social structure ... And we find our beliefs easier to maintain when some around us believe as we do. We might call this the "social component of belief" ... We can aid our students by coming alongside them in the midst of their tensions. When we do, we shift the locus of integration by implicitly inviting them to continue their struggles, not alone, but within the relative safety of the faith community.[129]

It is no secret that the metaphor of the body used by Paul in the Second Testament indicates a unity of community. The church is the best place "to receive the kind of teaching that encourages and deepens faith."[130]

Jesus, in his high priestly prayer (John 17), was most concerned that believers would maintain a disciplined unity of belief. Doctrinal solidarity with other Christians is paramount in the early church mission statement of Acts 2:42–47. Christian communities were marked by repetitious words like "one," "body," "others," "one another," and "members," such as is found in Romans 12:3–10. The English word itself makes the point: there is no community without *unity.*

Aquinas'[131] teaching was a reflective, communitarian response that arose from the love of truth, God, and humanity. Indeed he said, "A man needs the help of friends in order to act well, the deeds of active life as well as those of the contemplative."[132] Completing a cohort PhD program, I know firsthand the importance of camaraderie in the battlefield of ideas. Not only did I investigate hundreds of sources, listening to voices past and present, but my compatriots and I also studied together. Learning in community: another key to discipline.[133] In the firefight of ideas, I say with those joined in battle, "I love those guys."[134]

Discipline: School This Fool

The best defense against error is the offense of truth.

I go through violent withdrawal after football season. Trauma begins when I tune in to CBS or Fox on Sunday afternoon only to find cameras fixated on professional basketball or golf. So it was with great joy that I received an assignment from a football coach who wanted me to find problems with his team's offense. "I need quality control," he began. "You know football. I need you to be another pair of eyes on the field."

Consultation, an external overview of an organization's practices, is a booming business. Companies concerned with corruption or improvement hire firms whose task it is to provide unbiased observation. Auditors oversee bank business. Independent examinations maintain compliance for tax attorneys. Newspapers have ombudsmen to scrutinize the news. Patients get second opinions after one doctor's diagnosis. TSA personnel scour baggage and wand passengers prior to airline departures. Quality control in manufacturing can be seen attached to purchases from department stores: "This garment checked by inspector #9." Diamonds are appraised. Homework is graded. Inventories are inspected. Oversight is culturally woven in our eyesight.

But we cry, "Who are *you* to tell *me?*" We hate outside authority in our personal lives. Americans tend to agree with our country's first flag: a snake was segmented into thirteen colonies with the caption "Don't tread on me!" Yet our national hypocrisy is clear when we believe the latest chatter from talk show hosts or listen to a Hollywood actor's political views.

Authority upon which middlebrow culture rested is gone, replaced by celebrity. Criticism, once a profession with gatekeepers, is now the enthusiastic avocation of anyone with an Internet connection, and authority is bestowed by sales figures, not deans of culture … Technology has trumped teleology, and when we feel the need to assuage our feelings of cultural inferiority, we don't buy fifty feet of books. We buy an iPod. We are keen to signal our mastery of information, which has replaced knowledge as our cultural currency, and the idea of mastering the Western canon seems quaint in an age that publishes books with titles such as *How to Talk About Books You Haven't Read*.[135]

Leo Tolstoy is famously credited with bridging the need for authority and the desire for individual autonomy: "Everybody thinks of changing humanity and nobody thinks of changing himself." No wonder Paul and Peter both prayed for and commanded "growing in the knowledge of Christ."[136] As Christians, we focus our need for outside assessment on inside conformity to Jesus.[137] This is what theologians refer to as "progressive sanctification." To tag current educational commercials, "The more we know, the more we grow."

Biblical knowledge should produce personal discipline arising from revelation.[138] Discipline gives instruction,[139] supervision,[140] and correction.[141] Discipline is marked by chastening or warning. Far from static, this is an action word—hard work won, a quality of character. It is used frequently with correction or reproof.[142] Discipline has a verbal rather than physical persuasion—an appeal to reason. The wise believer applies discipline to himself or herself, having learned a lesson.[143] Discipline must not be taken lightly, and it does not come easily.

Discipline beckons;[144] she never coerces or drags the person in, kicking and screaming. Most susceptible to being undisciplined are those whom Scripture terms "simple." The Hebrew word—sounding very much like "petty" in English—means wide open to influences, whether good or bad. "Simpletons" acquire the label from something that is wide or open, spacious, vast, and abundant in capacity. They literally fall into trouble! Simple ones have a way of finding distress, since they are quite indiscriminating shoppers in the marketplace of life.

Proverbs 9:13 labels them as "silly," being devoid of knowledge. A few verses later, Solomon maintained the undisciplined lack judgment, sanctified savvy; they are unable to see through the facade of spoiled merchandise (9:16). Standing on the corners of choice and decision, the simpleton is unable to make up his or her mind.[145] Is there hope for the undisciplined? Unlike other words for "fool" in Proverbs, this individual has the potential of being reached for the good. Invasion and saturation of the Word soften his or her heart. Persistent, consistent teaching will school this fool.[146]

A need to know was the reason Daniel Boorstin claimed "man the discoverer" as his hero.[147] Humans' insatiable urges are likened to what football coach Vince Lombardi taught his players about winning: "You must have a flaming desire to win. It's got to dominate all your waking hours. It can't ever wane. It's got to glow in you all the time."[148] Proverbs 19:2 weds passion with knowledge. Our need for an outside source of truth cannot come from consultation companies or celebrity opinion. We need external truth—the revelation of Scripture—to capture our internal territory. We need the Spirit's quality control to channel our passions. Internal conformity to eternal authority—herein is discipline.

Discipline: Call of Duty

The game of life necessitates time spent in the intellectual weight room.

I love my country. My voice cracks when I sing the national anthem. Tears come to my eyes when an Air Force jet passes over a football stadium before kickoff. Seeing uniformed service personnel in airports, I walk over to shake their hands, thankful for their service. A smile lights up my face when I think of my students who serve in our military. No country is perfect. But for years, I've watched as people risk their lives to get from Havana to Miami for the privilege of our freedom. To my mind, living in this country is a privilege, bearing the weight of responsibility.

Paul Ray Smith, member of the legendary Rock of the Marne, Third Army Infantry Division, bore that weight with his blood. Sergeant First Class Smith received the Medal of Honor, having risked his life above and beyond the call of duty:

> Fearing the enemy would overrun their defense, Sergeant First Class Smith moved under withering enemy fire to man a .50 caliber machine gun mounted on a damaged armored personnel carrier. In total disregard for his own life, he maintained his exposed position in order to engage the attacking enemy force. During this action, he was mortally wounded. His courageous actions helped defeat the enemy attack, and resulted in as many as fifty enemy soldiers killed, while allowing the safe withdrawal of numerous wounded soldiers.[149]

Then-President George W. Bush presided over Smith's posthumous Medal of Honor ceremony, during which he said, "Scripture tells us ... that a man has no greater love than to lay down his life for his friends. And this is exactly the responsibility Paul Smith believed the sergeant stripes on his sleeve had given him."[150]

Responsibility to defend others in combat is born out of military discipline: a state of order, obedience, and responsibility in performing one's duty.[151] But we live in a culture where the response, "Who? Me?" forms the cornerstone of our internal edifice. "What? Take responsibility for my actions? Is that *legal?*" Bob Thaves, in his "Frank and Ernest" cartoons,[152] pokes fun at our inherent desire to pass the buck. Genesis 3:9–13 is the epitome of finger pointing. Adam and Eve's emphatic response[153] to God's questions is a guilt release. "Don't look at me!" or "That's not *my* problem!" or "I didn't know!" register our classic dodges. Lost is a sense of responsibility born of discipline bound by duty.[154]

For years, I have taught students that the twin pillars that uphold all the rest of life are gratitude and discipline. Without thankfulness, we acknowledge no authority outside of ourselves. Without discipline, we exercise no authority over ourselves. As a professor, I bear the responsibility of clear commitment to and communication of true truth.[155] My students are accountable for the privilege of learning and to the providers of that learning.[156]

Gregory Roper fell into the practice of beating himself up because those enrolled in his classes did not study. He gave his heart and soul to his subject and students. Yet he felt like an abject failure. It was not until he realized that his students were inherently corrupt persons who bore responsibility for their own learning that he began to come out from under the cultural-educational spell that "it's the teacher's fault."[157] Patrick Welsh, a public school instructor from Alexandria, Virginia, entitles his article, "For Once, Blame the Student."[158] Welsh compares American-born and immigrant students. The former have no sense of gratitude because of entitlement; the latter discipline themselves to accept more work for more learning.

"Why do I have to do this?" Similar cries can be heard in both home and school. Scripture teaches that we are unwilling to learn, because we are sinners. After Adam's sin, God told humanity that work would be difficult.[159] Schoolwork is no exception. Christian teachers should know that our natures are the largest roadblocks to education. Molding the character of the student, then, becomes key to how children develop academically. If I recognize that sin has tainted all of life, this galvanizes my resolve, prompted by the Spirit,[160] to overcome the difficulties of learning with hard work.[161]

If we believe people are inherently corrupt, we believe that education begins with character development—the interiority of the person—not with programs intended to address external issues of concern. This view holds personal responsibility as paramount for what we do, no matter our race, nationality, or religion. Talk with any military personnel, and he or she will say the same: discipline arises out of responsibility to do one's duty. It was Sergeant Smith's personal discipline that motivated duty to country and the lives of his soldiers. Discipline, our willingness to sacrifice for others, demonstrates proper Christian response to my commander in chief—the King of glory.[162]

Holiday: Thanksgiving, Androcles and the Lion

Holidays offer us time to study the most important life issues.

Androcles, a young Roman slave, sought escape in the wilderness from his unhappy life. Finding respite in a cave, he found himself face to face with a lion. The beast was anxious only for the removal of a thorn from his paw. Upon its extraction by Androcles, the lion submitted to the man, caring for him. After being captured as a runaway some time later, Androcles was sentenced to death by mauling within the coliseum. However, the lion let loose upon Androcles was one and the same who had benefited from the slave's earlier kindness. Instead of attacking the defenseless man, the lion lay at his feet, whereupon both were released by an astounded Roman governor.[163]

Aesop's "Androcles and the Lion" prompts reflection on Thanksgiving. What should be our response to external grace? To whom do we say "thank you"? How does thankfulness change us? John Wilson's review of Alexander McCall Smith's latest novel *The Lost Art of Gratitude* suggests "McCall Smith … has created a fictional microworld to highlight aspects of the ungraspable Real … of our common life … the reader—savors the pleasures of food and companionship, the wonder of a child, the haunting presence of Brother Fox … And all this moves [the heroine] to immense gratitude, which the book itself unashamedly urges on us as well."[164]

Scott Cairns' "Thanksgiving Poem" sparks our collective awakening to thanks which produces "widespread and pervasive … giddy gratitude I recognize."[165] Peggy Noonan, America's essayist-laureate, recounts the gratitude of

> A friend who emigrated from Nicaragua twenty-one years
> ago and lives now in New York knew right away what she

was thankful for: her still-new country. "I'm mainly grateful that I could raise my son in freedom. I could vote for the first time in my life. I could express my opinions without being shot on the spot, jailed, or exiled like my grandfather. I could sleep through the night without fearing for my life. I could work and buy food without rationing."[166]

Roger Scruton reminds us that Americans in 2006 were far and away the largest private contributors to charities worldwide. He warns, however, that when government programs take over meeting the needs of people that "gifts are replaced by rights, so is gratitude replaced by claims. And claims breed resentment."[167]

Not beholden to governments, we are beholden to each other. Thankfulness is the recognition that our fullness comes from caring people outside ourselves. W. H. Auden wrote a multisection poem "A Thanksgiving for Habitat" that connected his physical home with personal friends. Each room, event, and remembrance is directly linked to anticipation of renewing human bonds. My favorite, tear-stained stanzas include

> Easy at first, the language of friendship
> Is, as we soon discover,
> Very difficult to speak well, a tongue
> With no cognates, no resemblance
> To the galimatias [gibberish] of nursery and bedroom,
> Court rhyme or shepherd's prose,
>
> And, unless often spoken, soon goes rusty
> Distance and duties divide us,
> But absence will not seem an evil
> If it make our re-meeting
> A real occasion. Come when you can:
> Your room will be ready.[168]

"The lines have fallen for me in pleasant places; indeed I have a beautiful inheritance."[169] God's goodness to us is our ultimate change agent. Ecclesiastes compares "life as a gift of God" with those who only see things "under the sun." The refrain that runs throughout the book[170] establishes the baseline barometer for human purpose. Solomon calls to his readers for a shift of mind-set.[171] For believers in the personal, eternal, triune Creator, mind-set shift is first upward, then inward, then outward.

To acknowledge life as a gift of God, one's whole focus and concentration must be moved from ourselves to One outside ourselves. Disciples of Jesus as Lord bow the knees to their sovereign Savior, both in response to who He is as well as what He has done. Appreciation is born out in worship.[172] Our love for God through others[173] brings joy in our God-given lives. "Androcles and The Lion" teaches the lesson: thanksgiving in this life begins by looking up, changing within,[174] and giving out.[175]

Holiday: Thanksgiving, Crawling over Broken Glass

What am I willing to do to show my gratitude for God's grace?

"It's wasted on a generation of spoiled idiots." Comedian Louis CK believes this is the response of many who live in an amazing world. "New York to L.A. takes five hours. It used to take thirty years. By the time you got to California, you were with a whole new group of people." Complaints about air travel? "You hear people say (in a whiny voice), 'I had to wait twenty minutes to board the plane.' Oh, really? You're sitting in a chair in the sky! You are flying through the air!" Is your cell phone too slow? "It's going to space! Can you give it a second?" Watching YouTube videos of CK's stand-up or late-night talk show appearances reminds us that we expect too much and are too seldom thankful.[176]

Michael Douglas plays such an ingrate in *The Game*. Douglas' character, Nicholas Van Orton, has everything; but like Scrooge, he appreciates nothing. He lives in opulence yet has cut himself off from every relationship that matters. Sean Penn plays Douglas' brother, who gives him an interactive game experience for his birthday. Initially unimpressed, Douglas goes along, unaware that he is being drawn into series of debacles that will overturn his life. The viewer is given the same ride. We are dragged through a world impossible to predict. Crisis upon catastrophe is piled high. Every fright is replaced by another horror. Just when we think the character can take no more, the tension is ratcheted up another notch. Our initial revulsion at Nicholas Van Orton is upended at the end as we see him broken, uttering the phrase "thank you" for the first time. And then, if we are sensitive to the story, we no longer see actors but ourselves.

How often do we bellyache about the slightest of grievances? Did another driver cut us off on the highway? Was someone inconsiderate in the checkout line? Did a person not meet our slightest expectation? What small inconvenience has intruded upon our lives today? Has a light bulb gone out? Has the printer run out of ink? Did we get a paper cut? Were we let down because the product was out of stock? Were our lattes not made to our liking? Are we a generation of whiners? Are we ever pleased about anything without qualifying complaint? Can we stop focusing on the smallest of maladjustments from our day to consider our ingratitude? Have we become Scrooges?

"He is a wise man who does not grieve for the things he has not, but rejoices for those which he has" is wisdom ascribed to the Greek philosopher Epictetus. "Gratitude is not only the greatest of virtues but the parent of all others," says the Roman historian Cicero. Seneca, Cicero's contemporary, adds, "He who receives benefit with gratitude repays the first installment on his debt." And Dietrich Bonhoeffer—a man who could make this claim based on how he lived—wrote, "In an ordinary life we hardly realize that we receive a great deal more than we give, and that it is only with gratitude that life becomes rich."[177]

To be thankful is to acknowledge someone outside of ourselves. What we need is confession, the essence of the word for "thankfulness" in Hebrew. We tend to think of going to confession to ask forgiveness for sin or giving a confession of guilt before a court of law. But the First Testament term emphasizes a declaration of God's greatness. Exaltation, praise, or glorification, remembering God and His works, are confessions.[178] Our confessions are to be made among the nations and in large assemblies of people with song.[179] Confessional praise was to be wholehearted with a right mind continually.[180] Indeed, Jesus came from Judah's line, whose name means "to confess."[181]

G. C. Berkouwer takes gratitude to its ultimate level: "The essence of Christian theology is grace, the essence of Christian ethics is gratitude." Doing right is proper confessional reaction. Doing right is based on remembering we live before another. Doing right is a small response to a large endowment. Second Corinthians 9:15 summarizes what should be our singular feedback, "Thanks be to God for His indescribable gift!" R. C. Sproul answers, "Once we have received this grace of eternal life in Jesus Christ, we should be willing to crawl over broken glass to honor and praise Him for that grace."[182]

Ethics courses should be built on confessional praise, thereby reminding us all we have come from someone else. Louis CK is correct: we should take nothing for granted. Our first thought should be, "How providentially fortunate I am to be living now, enjoying the goodness of this life." This is what George Bailey (Jimmy Stewart) discovers in *It's a Wonderful Life*. When we think our impact is insignificant, we should think of Frank Capra's classic tale. Let us take stock of our lives. Stop whining. Celebrate the large blessings over the small evils. Content ourselves with what we have, not what we want. May we find ourselves at the end of the tale in the lives of Nicholas Van Orton and Ebenezer Scrooge. And may we thank Christ that we even have the opportunity.

Holiday: Christmas, "I Murdered Them All Myself"

Every mystery writer depends on sin for the plot.

Still-beating hearts and walled-off living victims were the subjects of Edgar Allen Poe's macabre tales.[183] Poe was my favorite writer in junior high. I mentioned this once while speaking at a conference. A well-meaning soul sought to explain the gospel to me on a comment card, not believing that someone could be a Christian and love Poe at the same time. There is a reason why humans are drawn to the classic suspense genre, but it was not until I was an adult that I understood the reason for my strong attraction to Poe. What draws us toward the unknown? What is it that stirs our hearts to mystery? And why ponder Poe at Christmas?

"Can you keep a secret?" is the question of mystery. The English word has given us the process of initiation. A secretive ceremony honors the first-time participant. In our culture, the word "mystery" has come to ask the question, "How will this crime be solved?" TV dramas inevitably answer the query in an hour's timeslot. But once the case is cracked, there is no more mystery. While detective stories may baffle us, eluding our understanding for a time, the narrative has a conclusion. The older word "mysterium" better explains the original intent of the term. Mysterium marks the location, physical or otherwise, where something obscure takes place.[184] The opening line of the old radio show says it best: "You are now entering the inner sanctum."

Friday the thirteenth seems to present a mysterium problem for emergency room doctors. Atul Gawande recounts his thoughts about the event in his award-winning book *Complications: A Surgeon's Notes on an Imperfect Science*.[185] Gawande states that there is no immediate explanation for the excess number of ER visits on a day marked by superstition. While a committed natural science researcher, neither he nor other doctors could explain the abnormal increase in hospital needs on that fateful calendar day. The evidence, however, did not seem to suggest to physicians a supernatural answer: it was nothing more than a fluke. But, unable to catch a break or keep the patients straight on one such Friday, Gawande began to wonder why that day presented more problems than others. A nurse explains, "It's a full moon Friday the thirteenth." Gawande narrates, "I was about to say that, actually, the studies show no connection. But my pager went off before I could get the words out of my mouth. I had a new trauma case coming in."[186]

P. D. James, the famed British detective novelist, was asked why her specific craft so engages our minds and imagination. Because her books are often tied first to a homicide, James responds, "Murder is the unique crime, the only one for which we can make no reparation, and has always been greeted with a mixture of repugnance, horror, fear, and fascination. We are particularly intrigued by the motives which cause a man or woman to step across the invisible line which separates a murderer from the rest of humanity."[187]

"I had murdered them all myself."[188] Father Brown perhaps comes closest to true, biblical mystery. While a crime may have been solved, the good padre still wondered after the human penchant toward sin. Sherlock Holmes fans are used to deductive reasoning: a scientific analysis, assessing problems from the outside in. Father Brown *became* the murderer because he *was* a murderer. Chesterton's sleuth, a Catholic priest, saw people as they were, from the inside out. The mystery of our own nature continues: "The heart is hopelessly dark and deceitful, a puzzle that no one can figure out."[189]

Flannery O'Connor believed that Southern authors were both "grotesque" and "Christ-haunted."

> We find that the writer has made alive some experience which we are not accustomed to observe every day ... If the writer believes that our life is and will remain essentially mysterious, if he looks upon us as beings existing in a created order to whose laws we freely respond, then what he sees on the surface will be of interest to him only as he can go through it into an experience of mystery itself ... Such a writer will be interested in what we don't understand rather than in what we do.[190]

O'Connor exactly represents the New Testament word for "mystery." The secret thoughts and plans of God, formerly hidden, are now revealed. In no way is the mystery diminished. We still wonder at God-perpetrated events. So-called mystery religions kept mysterious teachings they did not wish to fall into unworthy hands. The group controlled the available knowledge, requiring all to become initiates. Christian mystery, on the contrary, is freely proclaimed to the world.[191] The Christ hymn of 1 Timothy 3:16 clearly announced belief in Jesus' life as being both historical and revelational. Jesus came in flesh, was vindicated by the resurrection, and ascended into heaven. His work was broadcast, believed, and became doxology. "This Christian life is a great mystery, far exceeding our understanding, but some things are clear enough."[192]

Christ's person and work are why I have a fascination with Poe. What is so attractive about mystery? How am I at once repelled by and attracted to what I find baffling? The unknown makes knowing the known possible. I crave mystery. I am fascinated by what I do not understand, which makes what I do know much more wonderful. Herein is the wonder of Christmas—the mystery of God becoming man.

Holiday: Christmas, Slaughter of the Innocents

Christmas cards true to Scripture would be soaked in blood.

Myths, falsehoods, and exaggerations crowd the covers of greeting cards every December. Here are a few. Xmas does not necessarily eliminate Christ from Christmas. X is the first letter of Christ in Greek, used as a symbol for Jesus. Santa Claus is actually based on a person in church history whose name was Saint Nicholas. Jesus was most assuredly not born on December 25. Mary did not ride on a donkey. The inn was not Motel 6 but rather reference to someone's home. A stable or barn is a modern explanation of a cave. A manger was a feeding trough for cattle, probably hewn out of the cave's rock floor. Three Magi seem to be based solely on the number of gifts given celebrating Jesus' birth. These and other fictions about Christmas arise from extra-biblical sources such as Christmas carols. We can say this for sure: "All was calm, all was bright" it was not.

Jesus' birth story[193] reads more like a reality detective show. He was born, as we would say, out of wedlock. "Unplanned pregnancy" is putting it mildly. In addition to the stigma of supposed premarital sex, Mary gave birth while she was on the road. The first witnesses of Christmas were from the lowest rung of society—shepherds. Scholars who should have followed the events did not seem to care. Yet astrological signs made pagan sorcerers caravan hundreds of miles to follow a star. Angels could not help themselves but exclaim. And then the bad guys showed up, and things got really interesting.

From the beginning, Jesus encountered threats against His life. The palace enlisted the aid of foreign intellectuals to locate the baby. When outsiders outwitted the king, he dispatched shock troops to find and kill the child. Warnings came through dreams. The family narrowly escaped to a foreign country. Ancient prophecies were fulfilled. Joseph—the silent type, male hero who did not utter a word—is the action figure responsible for Jesus' safety. From a human perspective, God's entrance into the world could not have been more mismanaged or more exciting. But with the infant came infanticide.

In a world of 24/7 news coverage, we are used to genocide. We sit, reclining comfortably, watching the horrors on our television screens. And then we change the channel. Were we to live under the authority of megalomaniac despots, we would better understand Jesus' birth. William Barclay gives us a thumbnail sketch of the tyrant at the time.

Herod was a master in the art of assassination. He no sooner came to the throne than he began by annihilating the Sanhedrin, the supreme court of the Jews. Later, he slaughtered three hundred court officers out of hand. Later, he murdered his wife, Mariamne; her mother, Alexandra; his eldest son, Antipater; and two other sons, Alexander and Aristobulus. And in the hour of his death, he arranged for the slaughter of the notable men of Jerusalem.[194] "Better to be Herod's pig than his son" became an apt proverb.[195] To target crown-claimers is one thing; to kill babies is another altogether. Genocide was perpetrated against defenseless innocents in Herod's attempt to kill the One of whom ancient prophecies foretold. Death and destruction were part of Jesus' birth.

Attacks on Jesus did not begin in Matthew. As "the ruler of this world,"[196] Satan has shed blood repeatedly over the millennia to wipe out the messianic line. Since Cain, who gave Steinbeck the storyline for *East of Eden,* the ancient serpent has attacked relentlessly.[197] The unnamed Egyptian pharaoh's death sentence was stopped dead by two named Egyptian midwives.[198] Starvation and death forced a Hebrew woman to include foreigners into her family, only to open Messiah's genealogy to Gentiles.[199] Inept planning by Haman was undermined through palace intrigue by Esther, a closet Jewess. Follow the pattern through the ages, and we discover murderous plots and purges against God's chosen people who would bear and bless Messiah.[200] Evil intentions never catch heaven unaware.[201] Unfortunately, extermination practices against the child mean that children will always suffer.[202]

Jolted to remember that the entrance of God in flesh is the central chapter in the supernatural battle, we must begin in Genesis 3. The whole of the First Testament anticipates his coming. Matthew and Luke took up the narrated story—something akin to *Law and Order* or *The Closer.* Blameless people died. Evil seemed to triumph. But then the tables were turned. An authority figure appeared. The bad guys lost. First John 3:8 is a verse that summarizes it all: "The reason The Son of God appeared was to destroy the devil's work." The slaughter of the innocents will never adorn the front of a Christmas card: but it should.

Holiday: Christmas, the Scrooge in Us All

If we thought about the need for Christmas,
we would put away the decorations.

I$\,$*Can Do Bad All by Myself.* Tyler Perry's film title speaks for itself. William Golding's *The Lord of the Flies* declares that humans can display what they are—inescapably, terribly dangerous. As Ralphie, the bespectacled target of power gone mad, says, "I'm afraid of us." The cold war strategist George F. Kennan would put it, "The fact of the matter is that there is a little bit of the totalitarian buried somewhere, way down deep, in each and every one of us."[203] Often I tell my students as I point around myself, "The problem is not *out there*." Then I point to my chest. "The problem is *in here!*"

"No man's really any good until he knows how bad he is." Father Brown knew what it was to be inside a man.[204] Alexander Solzhenitsyn's "Ascent," one of the autobiographical sections of Solzhenitsyn's *Gulag Archipelago,* justly asserts that "The line separating good and evil passes not through states, nor between political parties—but right through every human heart."[205] *The Strange Case of Dr. Jekyll and Mr. Hyde* by Robert Lewis Stevenson demonstrates the titanic battle raging within humans: depravity triumphing over dignity.[206] *How the Grinch Stole Christmas* is Dr. Seuss' classic tale about a hard-hearted creature whose life is obsessed with blotting out Christmas. Charles Dickens' *A Christmas Carol* reminds the softened soul that indeed, Scrooge lives in us all. Truth be told, we all have bad hearts.

But it's Christmas! We do not want to dwell on such things! We would rather, with our culture, declare ourselves good simply because we believe in something. Father James Martin, a Jesuit priest, exposes the siren call of consumerism for what it does and how we follow. Describing what he considers to be the most awful marketing promotions,

The winner of this year's worst catch phrase is a tie: between Macy's and Eddie Bauer. Macy's shopping bags say, "A million reasons to believe!" In what? What does Macy's want us to believe in? That Jesus is the Son of God? (Imagine that on a bag.) Nearly as maddening was the cover of this year's Eddie Bauer catalog, which proclaims "We believe." As with Macy's, I was eager to find out just what Eddie Bauer believed in. The Council of Chalcedon's fifth-century declaration that Jesus was fully human and fully divine? Not exactly. Page three professed the retailer's creed: "We believe in the world's best down."[207]

What is meant to be tongue-in-cheek condemnation of marketers is really a poke at us all. Who believes? We do! Why do we believe? Because down deep, we think we do good by giving. However, the mandate of gifts on a holiday does not a heart change!

But it's Christmas! Can't we rest on our goodness for one day out of the year? Backstory to our celebration on December 25 is an oft-forgotten character: Ahaz.[208] In his day, the world's superpower was Assyria, modern-day Iraq. Ahaz was king of Judah. Judah was a small nation state. When a couple of northern neighbors rattled their swords, Ahaz went looking for allies. Ahaz bet the farm on human partnership with Assyria's dictator, Tiglath-Pilesir III. Neither Isaiah's words of hope nor the Lord's direct communication swayed Ahaz from his human-centered course. Ahaz' small heart—the Grinch had one too, for a while—brought a frightening, foreboding, yet fulfilling prophecy to earth in Isaiah 7: "The virgin will be with child and will give birth to a son, and will call him Immanuel."

These words changed history. But because Ahaz's heart was proud, calloused, afraid, and shaken,[209] he refused to give the true Sovereign his trust. The Christmas story begins with king Ahaz, who forsook the true King.

But it's Christmas! Can we not tell a positive story? Why must we be reminded of our corrupt hearts? Our corrupt hearts make Christmas necessary. Without our need for a Savior, Christmas would simply retain its original intention—the pagan celebration of winter solstice. The Grinch and Scrooge repeat what our hearts need.

Every year, CBS runs the 1965 television classic *Charlie Brown's Christmas*.

And every year, people who watch hear Linus read the Christmas story from Luke 2, the result of Isaiah 7. Tyler Perry's movie is punctuated with preaching and ends with restoration. The Grinch is changed by good-hearted Whovillians who wholeheartedly believe in Christmas. Scrooge, confronting his past sins, falls on his knees in repentance. So I offer a simple poem to remind us of the Scrooges in us all—the possibility of change, because it's Christmas!

> Scripture informs
> Hearts are deformed;
> Until Christ, the heart storms,
> Salvation performed.
>
> The faithful are warmed
> By hearts conformed.
> When the Spirit reforms,
> My life is transformed.

Reading: Hammering on My Door

Words gain my attention; their ideas sit me down.

When I am dead, those who open my books will find other books inside. It is there I rejoice, exclaim, argue, oppose, join with, categorically deny, question, comment, and generally respond to the author. Add yet another reaction to reading comprehension—conviction:

> Behind the door of every contented, happy man there ought to be someone standing with a little hammer and continually reminding him with a knock that there are unhappy people, that however happy he may be, life will sooner or later show him its claws, and trouble will come to him—illness, poverty, losses, and then no one will see or hear him, just as now he neither sees nor hears others. But there is no man with a hammer. The happy man lives at his ease, faintly fluttered by small daily cares, like an aspen in the wind—and all is well.[210]

Anton Chekhov's short story "Gooseberries" captures conviction, his little man hammering away. It seems appropriate to begin a series on reading with the ethical purpose statement that books should change us. A manuscript ought to awaken my conscience, prick my spirit, send me to confession, and work both as cure and salve.

Louis L'Amour, an underappreciated adventure novelist, states clearly in his *Education of a Wandering Man*, "A book is less important for what it says than for what it makes you think."[211] A wide variety of authors concur with L'Amour. John Gardner says, "A brilliantly imagined novel about a rapist or murderer can be more enlightening than a thousand psycho-sociological studies."[212] George Bernard Shaw employs the metaphor, "You use a glass mirror to see your face; you use works of art to see your soul."[213] T. S. Eliot grasps a book's unconscious impact, "It is the literature which we read with the least effort that can have the easiest and most insidious influence upon us."[214]

Eliot's concern was well understood by Flannery O'Connor, who believes the book to be knocking on the door from the inside: "The novelist doesn't write to express himself, he doesn't write simply to render a vision he believes true, rather he renders his vision so that it can be transferred, as nearly whole as possible, to his reader ... Your problem is going to be difficult in direct proportion as your beliefs depart from his ... I have to make the reader feel, in his bones if nowhere else, that something is going on here that counts."[215]

"Comfort the disturbed and disturb the comfortable" is my favorite definition of preaching; it also seems appropriate for the conviction produced by reading. Consequences from the little man's hammer blows may sometimes be background noise, but the impact is always felt.

Children's stories continue to convict me, impacting my thinking. *The Little Red Hen* warns me against being a so-called friend who wants to take, not give. "The Sword of Damocles" compels me to be wary of desire for power. Rat and mole wander into the August presence in chapter 7 of *The Wind in the Willows,* teaching me both to fear and rejoice in the Almighty. *Yertle the Turtle,* the Dr. Seuss classic, warns me away from pride, leading to a (literal!) fall.

My life has no transformation without hammering on my soul. In our day of 24/7 entertainment, none other than Mortimer Adler and Charles Van Doren remind me,

> Television, radio, and all the sources of amusement and information that surround us in our daily lives are also artificial props. They can give us the impression that our minds are active, because we are required to react to stimuli from outside. But the power of those external stimuli to keep us going is limited. They are like drugs. We grow used to them, and we continuously need more and more of them. Eventually, they have little or no effect. Then, if we lack

resources within ourselves, we cease to grow intellectually, morally, and spiritually. And when we cease to grow, we begin to die.[216]

Read or die. Perhaps the greatest example of hammering conviction can be found in Nehemiah 8. In the Old Testament, Hebrew people would often have God's Word read to them. After a long sojourn in exile, Judah was back in her homeland again. Language skills atrophied. Nehemiah had to translate and interpret Scriptural injunction,[217] contextualizing true truth for his listeners. "All the people wept as they heard the words of The Lord declared to them" (v 9); understanding the reading sent Israel away "with great rejoicing" (v 12).

Samuel gives us a firsthand account of truth knocking on the door. The prophet used the Hebrew word *shmah*, powerfully connecting with Chekhov's metaphor in "Gooseberries." *Shmah* occurs nine times in 1 Samuel 15. In the context, Saul was about to rebel against God for a second time. The English reader can pick up the narrative repetition by watching for the words "hear," "listen," and "obey."[218] *Shmah* records a threefold impact on the hearer. We recognize and understand the words being delivered through our ears to our brain. Listening communicates comprehension; we know what we should do with what we have heard. But the first two do not count if we do not enact the correct response of active compliance in the third place.

Robert Coles, in his must-read *The Call of Stories*, summarizes reading's import: "The gnawing irony persists that powerful poems and poignant prose can affect us, excite us, cause us to see more clearly, yet not deliver that daily hammer-blow Chekhov prescribed."[219] I hope that people do not have to wait until I'm dead to read my words; I hope I do not die before I act on them.

Reading: Ice Ax to the Frozen Sea

Words on a page are a sledgehammer to my heart.

A former student, now a PhD scholar in his thirties, asked me to send him ideas for biographies to read. After reminiscing, I wrote four single-spaced pages on books about people that had moved me. I ended my self-imposed assignment by telling the story of my reading Ernest Gordon's *To End All Wars* on a plane flight from Chicago to southern California while a professor at Moody Bible Institute. It was impossible to hide the tears that flowed while sitting among two hundred passengers in the fall of 2002. No other book in the last twenty years of my life has so impacted my person.

Alastair Gordon recounts his life-changing experiences that began with fellow captives practicing John 15:13. Australian, English, Dutch, Scottish and other allies suffered deprivation and death in the Wampo, Thailand Japanese prisoner of war camp. It was the "no greater love" of Jesus that began a chain reaction among the POWs who were being forced to build the Burma-Thailand railroad.

> Our regeneration, sparked by conspicuous acts of self-sacrifice, had begun ... it might be thought that, this [was a] change in atmosphere ... it was dawning on us all—officers and other ranks alike—that the law of the jungle is not the law for man. We had seen for ourselves how quickly it could strip most of us of our humanity and reduce us to levels lower than the beasts ... we were seeing for ourselves the sharp contrast between the forces that made for life and those that made for death ... love, heroism, self-sacrifice, sympathy, mercy, integrity and creative faith ... were the essence of life.[220]

Hope found exclusively in the Christian lifestyle of self-sacrifice changes people. Alastair Gordon reminds us, "Through our readings and discussions we gradually came to know Jesus. He was one of us. We understood that the love expressed so supremely in Jesus was ... other-centred rather than self-centred, greater than all the laws of men."[221]

"Heart surgery" in the biography of Alistair Gordon moved me. I want to read books that open my chest, operating on my affections. George Steiner agrees: "To read great literature as if it had upon us no urgent design ... is to do little more than make entries in a librarian's catalog." He then quotes a letter from Franz Kafka at twenty years of age: "If the book we are reading does not wake us, as with a fist hammering on our skull, why then do we read it? ... What we must have are those books which come upon us like ill-fortune, and distress us deeply, like the death of one we love ... A book must be an ice-axe to break the sea frozen inside us."[222]

Reading ice ax books should bust soul ice. At some point, a book should knock our socks off. Tears should flow. Assumptions must be reexamined, trite thinking trumped by tight thinking. Excitement then prompts others with the call, "Listen to what I just read!"

"Is not my word like fire, declares the Lord, and like a hammer that breaks the rock in pieces?"[223] Jeremiah 23:23–32 concerns prophets who do not tell the truth. God says His book shatters leadership lies that steer His people astray.[224] The indictment reaches a climax: "The burden is every man's own word, and you pervert the words of the living God."[225] God says His word, the hammer, will fall.[226]

The book that breaks rock should break us. I cannot think of a statement that more resembles a Christian in earnest study of Scripture, anxious for its application to life. Thomas Aquinas implores me from "A Prayer before Study" under the glass on my desk:

> Pour forth a ray of Your brightness
> into the darkened places of my mind;
> disperse from my soul
> the twofold darkness
> into which I was born:
> sin and ignorance.

Books worth our attention should be pickaxes to the frozen sea, our internal sin. But books that move us are impossible without God's book, His Word. Scripture shattered the culture of a prison camp with the love of Jesus. That story made me weep to see the Word in action. If Jesus were astonished to hear the story of one who acted on the authority of His Word,[227] how much more should I read books that swing the hammer?

Reading: Book Burning

Books should only burn in our hearts.

Indiana Jones and the Last Crusade patterned its book-burning scene after Joseph Goebbel's encouragement of Germans to incinerate volumes by Freud, Hemingway, Marx, H. G. Wells, and others in 1933.[228] Hitler is the often-vilified representation of totalitarian rulers,[229] intent on controlling information. Ray Bradbury's famous futuristic thriller *Fahrenheit 451* had its seed thoughts firmly planted in the horrors of World War II. Authorities send fire trucks to burn books in the classic tale warning against the loss of freedom.[230] Individuals counteract state power by committing books to memory, becoming walking libraries.

George Orwell wrote *1984* with the dread of Nazism also fresh in his mind. Slogans from the book's dictatorial party included, "Whoever controls the past controls the future. Whoever controls the present controls the past." O'Brien, the maniacal authority figure in *1984*, himself confesses to the need to regulate all cultural accounts and memories.[231] Both Bradbury and Orwell remind us that freedom of thought is tied directly to historical records.

Artillery shells scoring direct hits on the University Library of Bosnia in 1992 destroyed 1.5 million historical records—books, to be exact. American journalist Mark Danner, trying to understand the devastation asked the leader of the Bosnian Serbs, himself a published poet, asked, "Why attack a library?"

"Only Christian books were burned," was the horrific reply. "The others were removed." Dutch investigator of war crimes Jan Boeles maintains that "the cultural identity of a population represents its survival in the future ... [destroying a library is] the murder of a people's cultural identity."[232] Burning books rapes human intellectual heritage.[233]

"This is the first mass book-burning of the twenty-first century." So says George Thomas Kurian, editor of the four-volume *Encyclopedia of Christian Civilization.* Kurian continues,

> The set had been copy-edited, fact-checked, proofread, publisher-approved, printed, bound, and formally launched (to high praise) at the recent American Academy of Religion/Society of Biblical Literature conference. But protests from a small group of scholars associated with the project have led the press to postpone publication, recall all copies already distributed, and destroy the existing print run. The scholars' complaint? The *Encyclopedia of Christian Civilization*, they have reportedly argued, is "too Christian." "They also object to historical references to the persecution and massacres of Christians by Muslims," Kurian says, "but at the same time want references favorable to Islam."[234]

It would seem book-burning takes many forms. While there are those who intimate Christians are the group most noted for banning books, consider how Christian books are banned by not being mentioned in *The New York Times Review of Books*. One of my former students, a PhD in a large American university, told me recently that animosity toward Christians is growing. "There is an increasing lack of common ground believers have with nonbelievers."

Jeremiah 36 records an instructive event showing the age-old antipathy of unbelievers against God's people. Jehoiakim, confronted by God's Word, burned the scroll on which the Word was written. In marked contrast to his father, a good king of Judah, Josiah,[235] Jehoiakim and his officials did not show any fear or tear their clothes: a physical act to demonstrate repentance. Indeed, believing he could destroy the authority of the words by fire, Jehoiakim then sought to kill the human messengers of the Word.[236] Like many megalomaniacs before and after him, Jehoiakim's tyranny was marked by an attempt to eradicate the Word.

Falsification of Christian history has been the mode by which enemies of the church have attacked her historical record. Of all the religions of the world, only Christianity depends solely on the historical record for verification.[237] For years, I have taught my students this salient truth:

"If you begin to question a document's historicity, then you question its authenticity, and ultimately, its authority."[238] Since the first-century church was established, everything from Gnosticism to higher criticism to The Jesus Seminar to *The Da Vinci Code* has been used by our enemy to attack the historical record of Jesus and His bride. Christians must continue to fight for their historical heritage, the written Word.[239]

Jeremiah 36 reminds the Christian audience that the maintenance of historical records is imperative for the church. The famed Warburg collection of books—some eighty thousand volumes—escaped the reach of Goebbel's attempts to wipe out free speech by two weeks. The Warburg Institute built on the library to become an important part of the University of London's some 350,000 volumes today.[240] Salvaging history, sustaining ideas, saving words—the lessons of George Orwell and Ray Bradbury are enlightening. Free people everywhere fight to maintain their beliefs etched in stone, cuneiform, parchment, or paper.

Reading: Fire in My Bones

Words are only important if truth is important.

Theo van Gogh, a Dutch filmmaker, was shot dead by a radical Muslim two months after his film *Submission* was aired.[241] Showing the subjugation of women was too much for some in the Islamic world. Kurt Westergaard created the most famous of the Muhammad cartoons published in September 2005 in the *Jyllands-Posten* displaying the prophet with a bomb in his turban. Mr. Westergaard has been in hiding ever since.[242] Truth is on trial all over the world.

Dictatorial mind-sets loathe free expression of the individual. Napoleon's famed statement "Four hostile newspapers are to be feared more than 1000 bayonets" expresses universal despotic views. Lenin, intent on wiping out intellectual classes, birthed the twentieth-century practice of genocide.[243] Stalin hoodwinked Western cultural elites of the day to downplay the former USSR's mass murder of vocal opposition.[244]

Burning the authors of words seeks to eliminate intellectual heretics. John Wycliffe, who first brought the Bible into English, died of natural causes; yet his bones were unearthed, burnt, and scattered so as to eliminate his memory. Jon Hus was strangled and then burned for his attempt to communicate Scripture in his native Prague. William Tyndale had his life taken from him on the pyre while uttering the immortal words, "Lord, open thou the king of England's eyes." Tyndale translated Hebrew and Christian Scriptures into English against English law. Indeed, not a century later, the King James Version made his vision a reality. The problem for those who attempt to wipe out books at their source is a struggle to contain the impact of their martyrdom.

Eliminate the messenger or the message. Winston Churchill reminds us,

"A lie is half way around the world before truth gets its pants on."[245] Silencing jihadist critics via American higher education is endemic in academia today.[246] Thomas Sowell refers to the Western media—known as the Fourth Estate—as something more akin to a Fifth Column.[247] Former English Prime Minister Tony Blair coined the word "viewspaper" to indicate that the media no longer does "straight reporting"; rather, journalists create cynicism not by analyzing the results of one's judgments but his or her motives.[248] Josef Pieper was concerned that when words were divorced from reality, disassociated from truth, they would simply become "instruments of power."[249]

Kill the words. Kill words' meanings. Kill the wordsmiths. If it were not for international acclaim, freedom-loving writers such as Alexander Solzhenitsyn, Lech Walesa, Vaclav Havel, and Andrei Sakharov would have been butchered. Why are authors, playwrights, cartoonists, and intellectuals the first to be killed in totalitarian takeovers? Because words are power.

Acts 3:21 declares God to have spoken His Word through His holy prophets "since the world began." So Jesus condemned the powerful elite of his day in Matthew 23:31–35 because they killed the prophets: from Abel through Zechariah. Since Abel was killed by Cain in Genesis 4, the murdered "cry out to God."[250] In the end, "the earth will disclose her blood, and will no more cover her slain."[251] But the rider whose robe is dipped in blood will avenge all the Christ-following messengers, prophets, and wordsmiths returning to earth with Him.[252]

But *why* do words have power that force dictators to kill? "A fire imprisoned in my bones" is how Jeremiah 20:9 described the prophet's experience: he had to speak.[253] So changed by his conversion was Blaise Pascal that he wrote the word "fire" on a parchment he had sewn inside his coat.[254]

The fire of God's Word is truth. Truth cannot be denied, contained, overthrown, or destroyed. Dictators hate truth, because the truth sets people free.[255] One who personally lived the freedom of truth was Alexander Solzhenitsyn, the famed author of *The Gulag Archipelago*. He ended his acceptance speech for the Nobel Prize in literature by quoting the Russian proverb tyrannical types hate: "One word of truth shall outweigh the whole world."[256]

Reading: Better a Live Dog

Books describe life; the book explains eternal life.

Robert Fulghum, my favorite religious humanist, penned the title to end all titles with his *All I Really Need to Know I Learned in Kindergarten*. But it was one of his later tomes that most captured my attention.[257] Sitting in a chair beside his burial plot, Fulghum had himself photographed as he considered his final destiny. That picture hangs in his office as a visual reminder of his life's end. Astride his interpretations of Ecclesiastes 3:1–8 ("There is a time to be born and a time to die") are my comments reminding him of Ecclesiastes 3:9–15: "I know that there is nothing better for men than to be happy and do good while they live. That every man may eat and drink, and find satisfaction in all his toil—this is the gift of God ... And God will call the past into account." The humanist has here and now; the Christian has here, now, there, and then.

A few years ago, my pastor asked me to participate in a dialogue teaching. One of the questions for me to ponder and then recount during instruction on a Sunday morning had to do with why my vocation was important. I declared my belief that the education of young people was imperative because of our impending death. I am compelled to read, study, think, write, and teach, because my voice carries the voices of others to the next generation.

One of my favorite haunts in Grand Rapids, Michigan has closed. I used to wander through the basement of Kregel's looking for a bibliophile's book bargain. On one of my excursions, I remember distinctly stopping in my tracks, mid-stack. I was jarred by the thought, *These are dead men's books.*

I read dead men's books. Every day, I listen to the dead speak. I hear the words of Shakespeare and Poe. Auden and Milosz capture my attention. Stevenson and Shelley add their ideas. Moses and Luke give voice to history.

Dead men's words live today. As I think about how to live, I must first consider that I must die.

I think about death quite often. In fact, I would encourage all of us to consider our earthly demise more than we do. And I would ask us to hang metaphorical portraits of our gravesites on the walls of our minds. Ponder passages below that prompt us to not only consider that what we do in this life counts for the next, but also that our deaths ought to prompt our opportunities for living:

> Turn, O Lord, and deliver me; save me because of your unfailing love. No one remembers you when he is dead. Who praises you from the grave? (Psalm 6:5)

> He cut short my days ... so I said: "Do not take me away, O my God, in the midst of my days." (Psalm 102:23–24)

> Show me, O Lord, my life's end and the number of my days; let me know how fleeting is my life. You have made my days a mere handbreadth; the span of my years is as nothing before you. Each man's life is but a breath. Man is a mere phantom as he goes to and fro: He bustles about, but only in vain; he heaps up wealth, not knowing who will get it. But now, Lord, what do I look for? My hope is in you. (Psalm 39:4–7)

> Teach us to number our days aright, that we may gain a heart of wisdom ... May the favor of the Lord our God rest upon us; establish the work of our hands for us—yes, establish the work of our hands. (Psalm 90:12, 17)

"Better a live dog, than a dead lion."[258] I remember when my nephew, Ethan, got in trouble at school for quoting that as his favorite verse. But no other phrase from Scripture gives us better marching orders. Ecclesiastes 9:5 explains, "For the living know they will die, but the dead know nothing; they have no further reward, and even the memory of them is forgotten." Ecclesiastes 9:10, often misinterpreted,[259] completes the thought: while we live, we have opportunity—for here and now, there and then.

After playing Bruce Springsteen's *Glory Days*,[260] I remind my students that serving God should begin when they are young, as is taught by Ecclesiastes 11:7–12:1. Jacques Ellul well summarizes the truth: "Remember your Creator during your youth: when all possibilities lie open before you and you can offer all your strength intact for his service ... to serve as the presence of God in the midst of the world and the creation. You must take sides earlier—when you can actually make choices, when you have many paths opening at your feet, before the weight of necessity overwhelms you."[261]

Upper elementary school parents should read Katherine Patterson's *Bridge to Terabithia* to their children. Originally penned as a personal response to a young friend's death, Patterson's classic touches the cord of loss families feel at the graveside of a loved one. High school should prompt reading of Tolstoy's *The Death of Ivan Ilyitch*, where one discovers as he is dying that he never really lived. And as an adult, *As I Lay Dying*, penned by Richard John Neuhaus, is an important rumination teaching us how to live: all the more poignant since his own death.

When discussing the end of days, how does God end His book? By talking about how important are the words *in* the book! In English, we can see that "words" and "book" are mentioned six and seven times respectively—a marker of their importance.

> "These words are trustworthy and true;" "Blessed is the one who keeps the words of the prophecy of this book. You and your brothers the prophets, and with those who keep the words of this book;" "Do not seal up the words of the prophecy of this book, for the time is near;" "I warn everyone who hears the words of the prophecy of this book: if anyone adds to them, God will add to him the plagues described in this book, and if anyone takes away from the words of the book of this prophecy, God will take away his share in the tree of life and in the holy city, which are described in this book."[262]

There are those who testify on behalf of the book.[263] The Alpha and Omega is coming, the first and last letters of the alphabet, the One about whom the book was written.[264]

I can hear the vocal complaint by any who read this essay: "What in the world has death got to do with *reading?*" Perhaps the idea is best summarized by a movie of which I never tire, *The Shawshank Redemption*. The theme, summary, reason for reading, and reason for doing anything while we live are uttered by Red (Morgan Freeman): "Get busy livin' or get busy dyin'."

Robert Fulghum is right to consider his gravesite every day. Better yet, we should remember the One who knows our grave days. Life is a gift from God. Enjoy it. Enjoy Him. Read a book.[265] Read God's book.[266]

Reflection: Hyper-schedules

We're too busy because we're too lazy.

"I think people are too busy to rest," one colleague declared to me. Another friend wrote the same week to say that her employer did not value retreat. As I considered both comments, I recalled that Lee Iacocca once said a company president who cannot take two weeks off out of the year has no business running a business.[267]

There is a conspiracy of busyness[268] in our culture that allows little time for people to plan, organize, or practice collaboration.[269] The phrase "I don't *have* the time" versus "I don't *take* the time" differs by one word, spanning an ocean of meaning. What a culture values shapes the values of people in the culture. American culture has an inbred Seabee mentality that "We can do it" that has morphed to the Nike slogan "Just do it." Western values are premised in achievement, in doing.

"The Unbusy Pastor"[270] by Eugene Peterson is a chapter I encourage my students to read once a month. Peterson confesses that his busyness is linked directly to his vanity and laziness. In the first place, Peterson says we find our worth and significance in how much people need us. Our hyper-schedules are proof that we are important. His second point is confirmed through paradox: we are lazy because we allow others to set our workdays for us. We sacrifice what is most valuable to us—our time—by spending it on pursuits that may be outside our personal, God-given missions.

We believe that what we do tells who we are. Some of our works-righteousness mentality began with clocks. Daniel Boorstin gives a brief but powerful history of clocks in *Cleopatra's Nose: Essays on the Unexpected.*

> Inventions redefine experience ... The inventing and
> manufacturing of clocks created the need and demand

for clocks. Until lots of people owned or had access to timepieces there was obviously little need for anyone to have one. Why be there "on time" if nobody else was? ... The young United States of America attracted the wonder of the world with its cheap dollar watch ... and it was no accident then that this also became the land of the quick lunch and of young men in a hurry.[271]

There are two methods of knowing what is important to people: where they spend their money and how they spend their time. We have allowed our creations to control us. Born of our dedication to clocks, getting things done has become our cultural imperative.

Reflection can reclaim time. Reflection is a term that originates with Hebrew words for "meditate." The sound of one word gives the impression of a murmur, sigh, whisper, or moan.[272] On the one hand, there is a sense of the darkened, smoke-filled room used for hatching wicked schemes;[273] on the other hand, the righteous are to deliberate over proper answers.[274] The two-sided coin of reflection is nowhere better shown than in a comparison between Psalm 1:2 and 2:1: "the righteous *meditate*" and "the wicked *plot*," "meditate" and "plot" being the same word in Hebrew. Reflection begins as an internal process.

So Psalm 19:14 captures the most famous reflective statement, "Let the meditation of my heart be acceptable in your sight, O Lord."[275] Silent rehearsal, turning something over in one's mind, ends in an enthusiastic, emotion-filled confession. The believer then rehearses God's works to all those around![276] Once the silent reflection is told to others, the teaching continues to talk to the reflective heart.[277] The process is to continue day and night,[278] focused on all God's works and words.[279]

What we reflect upon shows what is valuable to us. *Selah*, the repetitious word found throughout the Psalms, communicates value by its definition: to hang, weigh, or measure. The term was used in the Old Testament when people used scales to identify the cost or weight of an object.[280] How do we measure or reflect upon what is said in the Psalms? *Selah* is an interlude.[281] We are to stop, ponder, consider, and think.[282] We should pause for thought.[283] Take a break. Take a minute. Take a breath. Busyness should not be our business. Biblical reflection values the eternal over the temporal.

Reflection: Sometimes, I Just Sits

Take a seat, take a moment, take a look.

"Sometimes I sits and thinks, and sometimes I just sits." My sister, Jan, still reminds me of the phrase's importance. Emblazed on a poster that hung in our basement when we were kids, the words were accompanied by a rocking chair in the background. Jan quotes it from time to time. I have tended to smile, nod, and reminisce—until studying Psalm 77. The psalmist uses six different words in five different verses eleven different times for *think, consider, ponder, remember,* and *reflect.* Here the reader stops, sits, and thinks. In the case of this ancient song, the writer moans, a word that crescendos through turbulent times.[284]

"Would you like a little whine with that cheese?" is sometimes the response of some unfeeling souls who have suffered little. But for the afflicted, moaning turns to complaint and protest. Preoccupied with the hard situation, Psalm 77:3, 6, 12 uses the meditative word for one's pained response: a sigh.[285] But suffering is not one and done. Memories are dredged up from the situational cesspool. Better days are compared and found wanting.[286] Even so, at least his cries lead to a search.[287] And in the end, First Testament writers connect remembrance to reflection.[288] So how should we reflect on bad times, bad people, and bad situations?

Psychology, wrapped in Western pragmatism, desires to find an answer to our problems. Most analyses of our person by both Christians and non-Christians are centered in a works-righteousness perspective. We have to *do* something for resolution. Scripture, contrary to human-centered thought, finds us sitting without any other recourse but to wait. We *do* nothing. For a culture that "tends to value production over process," reflection assumes the need for quiet time "without the constant pressure to produce."[289]

In *The Wounded Leader,* Ackerman and Maslin-Ostrowski identify reflection as an alternative to action response. Writing one's story provides healing.[290] We need to get it out. The psalmist got it out, wrote it down, and expressed his thought, communicating the passionate purpose of his agony. "Some*times* I sits and thinks" is the importance of taking *time,* as the psalmist did, to write our narratives.

Significance also rests in noticing the first person singular all the way through the first part of the Psalm. "I cried," "I groaned," "I was too troubled to speak." Now notice the transition to the second person singular. The Psalmist decides, "It's not about me. It's about You."[291] Ultimately, we have no other recourse, no other answer, than to leave what we carry at "the court of appeals." It is the waiting that is most difficult.

Patience is not my virtue. But Rainer Maria Rilke has been slowly changing my mind.

> To await humbly and patiently the hour of the descent of a new clarity: that alone is to live one's art, in the realm of understanding as in that of creativity. In this there is no measuring with time. A year doesn't matter; ten years are nothing. To be an artist means not to compute or count; it means to ripen as the tree, which does not force its sap, but stands unshaken in the storms of spring with no fear that summer might not follow. It will come regardless. But it comes only to those who live as though eternity stretches before them, carefree, silent, and endless. I learn it daily, learn it with many pains, for which I am grateful: Patience is all![792]

If the artist and poet see waiting as ripening, how much more should I?! Christian theology is clear. There is a God. I am not Him. God is responsible for the story's conclusion. I am simply one of the paragraphs in His work.[293]

If "there is no measuring with time," as Rilke reminds us, then how do I read—much less write—about my life? We must "live as though eternity stretches before us." Rilke must have read Psalm 77:10: "Then I thought, 'To this I will appeal: the years of the right hand of the Most High.'" What strikes the reader is that the Creator has no years. He is eternal. Not only is 77:10 the center[294] of the Psalm, but also the only courtroom to which we can bring our cases so that they are heard. We cannot measure our circumstances apart from the eternality of God. The downside of this is that we may not know any conclusions, have any answers, or even see any justice in our years. And that is the point. There is nothing left to think about. There is no more reflection to be done. There is nothing left to say. Pull up a rocking chair, and have a seat. Look at the ways and works of God.[295]

"Sometimes, I just sits." My sister is right.

Reflection: Can't Live without It

When we wait, we hope.

It was midnight when she called. I heard the crashing of Lake Michigan waves mixed with Chelsea's emotions smashing against the shoreline. My daughter recounted a conversation she had had with a young atheist for whom her heart ached. She cried while explaining the fellow classmate's desire for something or someone to meet his expectation. For all her college years, Chelsea referred to herself as a female Apollos using the apologetic of hope with her peers. My daughter knows hope, lives hope, and gives hope to others.

In her *Mystery and Manners*, a writer's self-description, Flannery O'Connor explains the core of any good story, storyteller, and story-reader:

> People without hope do not write novels ... I'm always highly irritated by people who imply that writing fiction is an escape from reality. It is a plunge into reality and it's very shocking to the system. If the novelist is not sustained by a hope of money, then he must be sustained by a hope of salvation, or he simply won't survive the ordeal. People without hope not only don't write novels, but what is more to the point, they don't read them.[296]

Simply said, reality demands hope in a supernatural world. O'Connor's "A Good Man is Hard to Find," for example, causes one to gasp aloud in response to the depth of human sin and the necessity of divine grace. Hope to overcome the first is impossible without the second.

Hope is at the core of reflection. The Old Testament words for "hope" mean to look forward to with eager expectation.[297] Often translated "wait," Christians base their anticipation of the future in whom they wait. "Hope in God"[298] is the command based on the fact that Yahweh is "the hope of Israel."[299] Even Job in his agony declared, "Though He slay me, I will hope in Him."[300] "Wait for the Lord," the Psalmist said twice in Psalm 27:14, overloading the sentence in Psalm 130:5, "I wait for Yahweh, my whole person waits, I wait in His Word."

Why would we reflect if we have no hope, no expectation of someone or something beyond ourselves? Glenn Tinder masterfully exposes the bankrupt nature of human hope as so-called "progress" in his essay *The Fabric of Hope*. Likening a person's experience to an actor in a play, he says we know that there is a world outside ourselves on stage—that life transcends the drama. There is a world outside the theatre, so our hope is "An orientation toward eternity, presupposes a degree of detachment—the detachment inherent in the consciousness of belonging not only to an earthly city but to a heavenly city as well."[301]

Our troubles in this world cannot be overcome by empty political promises of hope that have no certainty, separated from history and transcendence. Micah 7:7 says what we mean: "I will wait for the God of my salvation; my God will hear me."

Hope can come in many forms but always comes from outside ourselves. Luke Wilson stars in a movie that helps us to ponder just such an idea: *Henry Poole Lives Here*. Sometimes the inexplicable occurs to give hope to the hopeless. Full of Christian imagery and truly caring believers, Henry is altered when he is forced to confront that which he cannot explain. After suffering his own devastating loss, Mark Pellington created a film to reflect upon the realities of life lived after loss.[302] *Henry Poole Lives Here* is an example of reflection leading to hope.

My preaching days began when I was thirteen. The first sermon I ever wrote began this way: "A person can live forty days without food, three days without water, five minutes without air, but not one second without hope." Here is to Flannery O'Connor, my daughter, and all those other apologists of hope. May their stories, poems, and films cause many to reflect and so to hope.

Reflection: Ordinary Order

The world, so large—mine, so small.

What is included in my journal seemed strange to me until I realized how much my writing reflected the Psalms. With the ancient hymn writers, I include recipes, incidents of my day, news items of warfare, reprinted prayers, agonizing cries, calls for retribution from God against my enemies, ponderings on the ways of humanity, opinions on international intrigue, joy in good things, poetry recitations, comments on the weather, remarks about creation, remembrances of historical events, or considerations over the obituary page.[303]

Musing: this word well summarizes the meandering drift of my Christian thoughts. "May my meditation be pleasing to him, for I rejoice in the Lord"[304] is the exact idea of another author some three thousand years ago. Today, we use the word "journaling" to communicate how we think when we write our reflections. The musings of the biblical author are not so different from my own. What I have come to realize is that what is termed ordinary is providential, ordained by God.

"Ordinary" is where we begin ("origin"), where we go to get our bearings ("orient"), or where find direction ("ordinance"). We arrange supplies, making lists ("ordnance"). We put first things first ("ordination"). We organize and systematize our lives ("order"). Ordinary order has come to mean what is regular or usual.[305] Alexander Pope stated, "Order is Heaven's first concern."[306] Duns Scotus referred to the distinctive nature of each individual thing as having "thisness"—a marker of creation's order. Richard Weaver's *Visions of Order* claimed that the inner order of the soul sustained the outer order of society.[307] Jane Jacob's *magnum opus*, *The Death and Life of Great American Cities*, argues for "visual order" in every metropolis.[308] All these examples reflect the original, ordered ordinance orientation ordained in Genesis 2:1: "Heaven and earth were finished, down to the last detail."[309]

Culture constantly craves newness. Order is overthrown for freshness. We now use trite phrases such as "nothing out of the ordinary" to communicate that zip, zero, zilch happened to us today. To this, Scripture is clear: even the animals understand the supernatural world. Isak Dinesen's description of her friend's supernatural view of everyday life is instructive in *Out of Africa*. Once awakened by her housekeeper to the harbinger of an all-consuming brush fire, the national explains, "I wanted to wake you up in case it was God coming." Gerard Manley Hopkins' "Glory be to God for dappled things" is a right Christian view of ordinary order. Who could ever forget, once seen, Rembrandt's etching in "The Good Samaritan" of a dog defecating in the corner of the picture? All of life is a celebration, a reminder of the natural, God-given creation. Of late, it has been Czeslaw Milosz who best captures ordinary order for me:

> "My parents, my husband, my brother, my sister."
> I am listening in a cafeteria at breakfast.
> The women's voices rustle, fulfill themselves
> In a ritual no doubt necessary.
> I glance sidelong at their moving lips
> And I delight in being here on earth
> For one more moment, with them, here on earth
> To celebrate our tiny, tiny my-ness.[310]

My journal celebrates the daily delights of "my-ness." Here are sample experiences I have lived during days of reflection:

- pondering turkey vultures, six-foot wingspans outstretched, perfectly still, sunning themselves in the early morning
- wondering at the majesty of a twelve-point buck jolted by my sudden appearance, bounding in six-foot-high leaps into the tall brush
- staring at early morning fog rolling across the fields
- walking on a frozen lake
- gazing at starlight blanketing the night sky, unpolluted by city lights
- watching purple martins zigzag through the air, eating their fill of mosquitoes

- admiring farm fields bursting green in the spring, harvest gold in the fall
- returning the donkey's brayed greeting when I walk past his outside stall
- marveling at long lines of pine trees placed in obvious rows
- fearing the pop-up storms that exploded across a springtime lake
- jaw-dropping sunsets defying description even with a full box of 128 Crayola crayons

Musing turns to music in Psalm 148, the reflections of ordinary order in my journal:

> Praise the LORD!
> Praise the LORD from the heavens,
> Praise Him from the heights!
> Praise the LORD from the earth,
> You great sea creatures and all deeps,
> Fire and hail, snow and mist,
> Stormy wind fulfilling His word!
> Mountains and all hills,
> Fruit trees and all cedars!
> Beasts and all livestock,
> Creeping things and flying birds!
> Praise the LORD!

Reflection: Out of Your Horn

One must put something in before anything comes out.

Eric Clapton's *From the Cradle* reverberated around the pool table as my son, Tyler, and I played one night. Clapton listened to the blues from a young age.[311] The blues couplets of loving and leaving, laughing and loathing, longing and languishing are both true at the same time. The blues is the perfect musical complement to reflection. As Charlie Parker pointed out, "Music is your own experience, your thoughts, your wisdom. If you don't live it, it won't come out of your horn."[312]

Steve Turner makes it clear that Negro spirituals are the soil from which the roots of blues, jazz, and even rock 'n roll get their nourishment.[313] It was the deep lament of slaves coupled with their high hope of Jesus' return that provided fertilizer for the blues. James H. Horn's *The Spirituals and the Blues* is an invaluable resource for understanding the history and theology of slave music in America. "The black experience in America is a history of servitude and resistance, of survival in the land of death. It is the story of black life in chains and of what that meant for the souls and bodies of black people. This is the experience that created the spirituals, and it must be recognized if we are to render a valid theological interpretation of these black songs."[314]

There is humanness in the blues, where pain and praise are partners. Life is messy. How we reflect about life[315] necessitates rough ground, a friction so we can walk, not slip. Slogging through the swamp gets us to the other side. [316] It seems that the most difficult lessons—those that take, lessons that matter, that move us on in life—are born of hardship and travail.[317] "The spiritual, then, is the spirit of the people struggling to be free; it is their religion, their source of strength in a time of trouble. And if one does not know what trouble is, then the spiritual cannot be understood."[318]

"Nobody knows the trouble I seen" is a verse born of travail, words from the birth canal of pain.[319] Reflection takes on new meaning when we give delivery to suffering. "Fly away and be at rest" is the song of those who hope for escape and relief.[320]

Bono of U2 fame has castigated evangelical Christians for their sick-sweet songs sung on Sundays. Worship music is too happy. It does not reflect the realities of life. Instead, Bono maintains, our vocal worship should sound more like the Psalms, which the rocker terms "the blues of the Old Testament."[321]

> But the spiritual is more than dealing with trouble. It is a joyful experience, a vibrant affirmation of life and its possibilities in an appropriate esthetic form ... The slave's view of God embraced the whole of life—his joys and hopes, his sorrows and disappointments, and his basic belief was that God had not left him alone, and that his God would set him free from human bondage. That is the central theological idea in black slave religion as reflected in the spirituals.[322]

"I reflected on all of this" is both a recurring and summary statement from Solomon in Ecclesiastes 9:1. "I thought to myself" and "I thought in my heart" are constantly repeated phrases in my favorite book of the Bible.[323] Leaving no stone unturned, life was "tested by wisdom."[324] Solomon declared, "Look, this is what I have discovered ... this is what I have found."[325] And what did he conclude? Ecclesiastes 8:15 tells us: "So I commend the enjoyment of life, because nothing is better for a man under the sun than to eat and drink and be glad. Then joy will accompany him in his work all the days of the life God has given him under the sun."

Here is Eric Clapton. Here are the slaves singing in the fields. Here is Bono. Here is the internal mark of longing on us all. Charlie Parker's reflection was right: "If you don't live it, it won't come out of your horn."

Obstacles: Boring

Boredom begins and ends with the person who is bored.

As a classroom teacher, I could always count on it. Once a year, like clockwork, some student in a new class would utter the infamous, vacuous student complaint against schoolwork. "That's *boring!*" Said pupil would hold out the "-ing" ending, trying to make as much as possible of a point from a two-word attack that one can make. As I mentioned, this happened once a year; and only once. The reason was my response: "The only thing boring about the subject is *you*."

Always met with a shocked expression, my Christian teacher retort allowed no reaction other than wide eyes and open mouths. "Considering the astonishing creation with which God has blessed us," I would begin, "nothing in the Creator's world is boring. Every subject is full of discovery. Every new piece of knowledge is a new opportunity. Every world wonder is worth a party. The problem with your negative remark," I continued, "is an assault on God and his world. But that's not all. Your comment tells the class that you think you know better about what you should learn. So here is your chance. Tell the class what you think we should be learning."[326]

An opportunity to defend themselves produced one of three student answers given over the years: "Nothin'" (accompanied by excessive pouting), "I just wanna have fun" (at least giving us something substantive to address), and "I want to learn about the real world" (mouthing an oft-used and sometimes accurate student lament).

"I don't wanna learn nothin'" is a lazy person's point of view. The underlying ideal within some teenage psyches is that someone else will live life for the person. Solomon was just as frank with his students as I was with mine. "How long will you lie there, O sluggard? When will you arise from your sleep?" Proverbs 6:9 demands accountability. I can hear the impatient[327] teacher speak to the slacker: "When you slack off someone has to pick up your slack!" The teacher is understandably irritated, according to Proverbs 10:26, comparing lazy people to smoke in the eyes and straight vinegar on the teeth. Laziness also "craves and craves."[328] Listless people long for, lust after, desire, covet, wish for, and get absolutely nothing.[329]

"I wanna do something fun" at least lets us explore what fun is.[330] Fun, to my students, was essentially, "I want to do what I want to do." Who doesn't? But Solomon likened this person to one who chases fantasies.[331] "Chase," in its Hebrew construction, means to persecute, hound, or pursue with abandon.[332] Picture a small child tricked into believing she could catch the shadows along the wall illumined there by her teasing sibling. There goes the little one, giggling, reaching for something that is not there! Not only is the student a child who wants only fun—something ephemeral, a momentary pleasure, a mist that lasts for an instant—but this pupil also wants what she wants and nothing else. But this scholastic situation is dire, as Proverbs 28:19 well summarizes: "Whoever works his land will have plenty of bread, but he who follows worthless pursuits will have plenty of poverty."

"I want to learn about the real world" is sometimes a shortsighted viewpoint. A long-range view is difficult with a short-range life. Teenagers have not lived long enough to behave responsibly with time. Young people do not have a sense that their real worlds now are those of going to school.[333] (It *is* important that teachers demonstrate the practical nature of their disciplines. A mathematics teacher should teach proofs and postulates as well as math habits and application.) Furthermore, the ant has many lessons to teach in Proverbs 6:6–11. Oversight is unnecessary: the insect is a self-starter (6:7). Foresight is essential, since the ant plans ahead, preparing for a time when preparation is impossible (6:8). Insight into the ways of the ant is crucial for the sluggard to learn her lesson (6:6).

Cornelius Plantinga answers that school is no holding tank where students await the great day when they emerge. Outside of the academy, people who hold full-time jobs use the phrase "the real world" because of the pressure they feel over business and life in general. In fact, Plantinga argues, if pressure is the real world, students know pressure *very* well! Every occupation can become a preoccupation. Working nine to five can be just as insular a life as cramming for tests and cranking out papers. Plantinga's point was that anyone can become so focused on her own life that she does not know the real world either. "Someone who lives in the 'real world' lives with an awareness of the *whole* world, because the *whole* world is part of the kingdom of God."[334]

"Don't you *see?*" I beseeched the new class. "I'm on your side! I want you to succeed! But you have to get rid of some of the—let's be honest here—*stupid* beliefs our culture peddles. We are made to believe by television sitcoms that we can have all the fun in the world without any consequences. Commercials assault our brain with the chorus, 'You can have it all and have it now!' And TV dramas give us the impression that our problems can be overcome in forty-two minutes (the real length of so-called hour-long shows)." My preaching reached a crescendo. "Don't believe the hype! Don't fall for the line! I want you to be wiser than your peers! All that we study is full of discovery and wonder. Boredom is for sluggards."

Obstacles: Twitching

We change technology so we don't have to change.

Icouldn't believe what I saw. A father walked his dog while his little boy tried to keep up. The young man attempted to get his dad's attention by pulling on his pant leg, but with no effect. Why? The man was talking on his cell phone. After numerous attempts to connect, the boy disengaged from his father, pulled out a small headset, hit the button on his recorder, and retreated to his own little world. I wanted so badly to tell this man that he was losing his son.

And schools are losing their students. My wife, Robin, is a second-grade teacher. If there is a drumbeat in some educational institutions, it is that we must give our students a technological edge. To what end? Robin contests, rightly, there is great access to information but little emphasis on comprehension. Schools can declare that they have attained a certain online standard (often assessed by the school itself). But an overload of information without understanding is simply more forgettable information.

Key to Twitter's success is having immediate knowledge. Twitter advertises the question, "What are you doing *right now?*" Information is supposedly "super fresh." Steven Johnson suggests in *TIME* that these details of life are not superficial but give depth to life. It may be true that celebrities can tell us about their causes and intimate, personal details. But it is difficult to believe that while the United States continues to show poor math skills from its school children, the number of communication gimmicks we have built somehow makes up for bad school scores.[335] No one complains about devices, for instance, that allow instant communication about anticommunist surges in Moldova, Egypt, or China. Twittering in church, however, makes another

TIME correspondent, Bonnie Rochman, concede, "The trick is to not let the chatter overshadow the need for quiet reflection that spirituality requires."[336]

Diversion is the reason people "cannot stay quietly in their own chamber."[337] Our desire for distraction has beaten in our collective hearts ever since Genesis 3. Norman Cousins put it this way:

> Our own age is not likely to be distinguished in history for the large numbers of people who insisted on finding the time to think. Plainly, this is not the Age of the Meditative Man. It is a printing, squinting, shoving age. Substitutes for repose are a billion dollar business. Almost daily, new antidotes for contemplation spring into being and leap out from store counters. Silence, already the world's most critical shortage, is in danger of becoming a nasty word. Modern man may or may not be obsolete, but he is certainly wired for sound and he twitches as naturally as he breathes.[338]

Twitter shows we twitch. Many complain that technology changes us. I suspect the opposite is true. We change technology so we don't have to change. Perhaps the more troubling idea is that I become easily distracted with electrons. My distraction is a pull toward the mundane, the inconsequential, and the vapid nature of whatever is new. Screwtape encourages his underling to use distraction to thwart the Christian at prayer.[339] A. J. Conyers argues that cultural inattention is a crucial component to distraction.[340] Maggie Jackson warns in *Distracted* that civilization as we know it is at stake.[341] In short, our attention is drawn toward the temporal over the eternal. Sin separates us from that which matters most. Our twitching began in the Garden.

"Is this the way it's supposed to be?"[342] the adversary questioned in Genesis 3:1. "Really?" "Are you *sure?*" The Hebrew construction of the serpent's speech accomplished two feats: the question temporalized the eternal Word, leaving open the option for human evaluation of the Word. The attack against humanity did *not* begin with a desire to become God. The attack was upon the Word of God. Once Eve was given the opportunity to assess God's Word, she *added* to God's Word: "or touch it" is not in the original Genesis 2:17 prohibition. Scripture twisting is now open to all comers. Placing the Word of God on the human level extracts Scripture's eternal origin, making the creature arbiter over the Creator. I would contend that we twitch because we want to twist the truth.

Bruce Waltke gives the necessary corrective. Our theological reflection must begin with the text.[343] The Bible always gives primacy to "word." "God predicts his actions and offers commentary before, during, and/or after the event, thereby asserting his role as the instigator and interpreter ... of the historical events assur[ing] a recognition of God's sovereignty over history, and the events are his vehicle of authenticating the truth he desires to communicate through them."[344]

Romans 1:18 tells us that when confronted by revelation, we "suppress the truth." Paul was concerned in Acts 20:30 that "from among your own selves will arise men speaking twisted things" intent on drawing disciples away. Second Timothy 4:4 maintains that sound teaching will be subverted, turning "away from listening to the truth, and wander[ing] off into myths." So this is Jesus' mission: John 14:6 declares that the Living Word is "the truth."

Truth is connected to relationship, a fact lost on the father who refused to give his son attention. We must listen to the right voices, speaking aright so others hear the truth. Study is consumed with the need for reliable information, not overload. Knowledge must be understood; hence the place of comprehension in learning. Study must connect us to what matters most— our need for the eternal Word. Our itch to usurp the role of interpreter, to become the arbiter of the truth, has ever since made us twitch.

Obstacles: Drifting

"And" does not unify; it divides.

"I'm going to mount *this* fish," declared the ten-year-old fisherman. We stared down at a sixteen-inch big mouth bass the young man had just caught in a small Indiana lake. The boy's plea to help take out the well-implanted hook from the animal's lip was an unusual diversion from my daily walk.

"How long have you been fishing?" I inquired.

"Since I was two; best sport in the world," my new acquaintance announced with resolution. This little man had hardly lived a decade and already had cornered one of life's keys: focus, resolution, dedication to mission.

"All you city folks come out with knots in your rope trying to figure out the meaning of life." Jack Palance interprets Billy Crystal's midlife crisis in *City Slickers*. Holding up one finger, he drives home the point to the clueless Crystal: "It's one thing. You find out what that one thing is." It is the one thing that drives people crazy. Until folks discover the focal point, they are destined to meander.

The phrase "mission drift" means that an organization has lost its focus. Taking a cue from NASA, leadership training indicates that the reason for a mission must be revisited every thirty minutes. Like space capsules, people in organizations tend to drift. Making sure that people remain committed to the original intention is crucial to the success of that institution. Small corrections in word, attitude, and action are needed constantly.

"Rudderless" is another word for mission drift. Caitlin Flanagan uses this word to describe California public schools in her February *Atlantic Monthly* article.[345] Close to one half of all California government schools

92

have adopted curricula that now teaches students how to grow their own nutritious food. Reading, writing, and 'rithmetic are supposed to be threads that run through the classes. But Flanagan quotes Theodore Sizer, founder of the Essential Schools movement, from his classic *Horace's Compromise*, "Some critics will argue that the school must go beyond language, math, and science to hold the interest of the pupils ... but a fourteen year old who is semi-literate is an adolescent in need of intensive, focused attention."

Enrichment programs, such as the California gardening craze, antismoking, or sex education, tend to push out supposed standardized curriculum. *The New York Times* reported that one-time Catholic schools that become charter schools in Washington, DC lose their original mission. Once religion classes anchored the school day and teachers readily turned to the Bible to reinforce lessons in the classroom. But no more. S. Kathryn Allen, a parent leader who protested the Catholic school closings last year, was quoted as saying, "When you change to a charter school, you are not allowed to do the things that make a Catholic school Catholic and that preserve our mission."[346]

Peggy Noonan asks important questions for every institution: "If you work in a great institution do you remember the mission? Do you remember why you went to work there ... what the institution meant to you when you viewed it from the outside?" Noonan concludes, "Turning around institutions is a huge, long and uphill fight. It probably begins with taking the one thing we all hate to take in our society, and that is personal responsibility."[347]

But what defines personal responsibility? Douglas Bowman's move from Google to Twitter caused quite a stir in the technology community. Bowman's ultimate decision was based on mission drift, which he defined by saying, "Without conviction, doubt creeps in."[348] *Without conviction, doubt creeps in.* Without conviction, distraction easily leads us astray. The courage of one's convictions keeps institutions on track. Convictions indicate someone has to care. Staying the course is a matter of conviction. Drifting off course happens when organizations do not constantly revisit their missions. The latest trends will soon be yesterday's news. One's mission must be based on the courage of one's convictions.

"As soon as you add the 'and' you've divided your mission."[349] I consulted with a school about its need for a philosophical framework. The well-meaning believers wanted to tell how they will help students emotionally, intellectually, spiritually, and physically, reducing humans to pie charts.

Each time we segment ourselves into pieces and parts, we transgress the wholeness for which we were made. Ever since Genesis 3, we have been intent on division. We divide from God by hiding—from ourselves, each other, and creational responsibilities. Maintaining unity within our person is difficult—seeing ourselves as one with Christ. Maintaining unity within a group of even well-intentioned Christians is more difficult still. Whether it be an individual or institution, finding and keeping focus is difficult.

When I think about obstacles to study, I think about loss of focus. There are many distractions that vie for my attention. Staying on course, avoiding mission drift, is hard. And then I remember my young fisherman acquaintance. He is resolute. He stays with fishing even when it's hard. I admire his commitment. He reminds me of Caleb, who believed God's promise about entering Canaan. Numerous Scriptures recount the same phrase: "Caleb had a different spirit; he fully followed the Lord."[350] May I have Caleb's spirit, for I am in constant danger of mission drift.

Obstacles: Using

What use is use if my life is useless?

"Useless eaters." Nazis coined the phrase for mentally ill patients. Indeed, the first people to die in the Holocaust were German World War I amputee veterans.[351] A naturalistic mind-set ("There is nothing outside of this world") births an evolutionary point of view ("Only the strong survive"). Then, a materialistic lifestyle ("Matter is all that matters") bends toward utilitarian ethics: personhood depends on productivity. What has worth must have immediate benefit.

Views of life centered on usefulness have a deleterious impact on education.[352] Neil Postman warns,

> In consideration of the disintegrative power of Technopoly, perhaps the most important contribution schools can make to the education of our youth is to give them sense of coherence in their studies, a sense of purpose, meaning, an interconnectedness in what they learn ... [However] There is no set of ideas or attitudes that permeates all parts of the curriculum ... It does not even put forward a clear vision of what constitutes an educated person, unless it is a person who possesses "skills." In other words, a technocrat's ideal is a person with no commitment and no point of view but with plenty of marketable skills.[353]

"When am I going to *use* this?" is the schoolroom mantra. Pragmatism—a desire for usefulness—subverts the need for building a broad understanding of all of life. Teacher conventions are noted for demonstrations and booths that unconsciously advertise the gnawing question, "Will it work?" On occasion, it seems that this is the only critical question teachers ask. Pragmatism works its wiles through teaching tips, recipes, and the call to "try this." The immediate and practical supplant vision and philosophy. But why is more foundational than how one practices education. Materialism spawns this deadly disease—where learning means earning—when the size of one's wallet is more important than the size of one's vocabulary.[354] Schooling becomes a means to an end. Do what you have to, and move on. Utilitarianism—the false belief that consequences of any action should provide production and pleasure—raises its ugly head.

However, "A society too commercial in orientation might lose its sense that there is anything higher than immediate gratification."[355] Consumerism, the offspring of materialism, is not the intention of creational law through human stewardship. Phrases such as "human resources," something to be used and used up, do not befit a Christian worldview. Business nomenclature, tactics, and ethos have made more inroads into the church than we would like to admit. Zenger and Folkman, for instance, regard changing attitude by changing behavior as high priority in *The Extraordinary Leader*. Again and again, the reader is told that behavior develops character—not the other way around.[356] Behavior modification, training a person's internal fortitude by external compulsion, seems to be the underlying belief. As a consequence, the real interest is in results.[357] Indeed, an earlier book from Zenger continues to sustain the theme: *Results Based Leadership*.[358] Performance, production, profit, and pragmatism drive the quest for success. While there is a genuine concern for developing and improving leadership, the ultimate measurement lies in the bottom line.

But when it comes to education, Proverbs is clear: knowledge is to be sought, acquired, and understood. Study is accomplished in stages.[359] Anything worthwhile takes work. Providential success is accrued over time, not overnight. Whatever we acquire, we have because God wills it.[360] Our ultimate goal is not for our own self-interests but the glory of God and the good of people.[361] *Telos* (Greek) is the Bible's word for end, fulfillment, or completion. Accordingly, Jesus is "the fulfillment of the ages" to which believers are to "hold firmly" with "diligence" and "perseverance," because He Himself is "the end."[362] Our interest is not in the bottom line but the end of the line.

George Peabody, widely acknowledged as the founder of modern philanthropy, gave millions of dollars in gifts toward educational causes in the mid-1800s. Why?

> Deprived as I was, of the opportunity of obtaining anything more than the most common education I am well qualified to estimate its value by the disadvantages I labour under in the society [in] which my business and situation in life frequently throws me, and willingly would I now give twenty times the expense of attending a good education could I possess it, but it is now too late for me to learn and I can only do to those that come under my care, as I could have wished circumstances had permitted others to have done by me.[363]

I once had a colleague in government schools who told me, "Mark, for the first time in ten years, I will be able to teach from the same curriculum I had last year." With our drive toward what works, we have moored our hopes to the sinking ship of "What use is it?" The mentality birthing the phrase "useless eaters" is subtly at work in educational corridors. Biblical wisdom in study prompts us to value people over productivity. Postman and Peabody knew the truth: our ends have longer lives.

Obstacles: Whining

Academic rigor is a student's responsibility.

Imagine a parent having just witnessed his or her son whiffing at the soccer ball, kicking at nothing but air. "Hey, stop the game!" the parent calls. "My son practiced so long and hard for this event! Give him a do-over!" I can hear you laughing now! Yet this happens at some point during every school's parent-teacher conference. "Johnny spent *so much time* on that assignment! His effort should count for something!"

Here is a story of one of the many times the "time equals grade" argument was proposed to me. "Imagine your son in welding class." I connected with a mom whose son took vocational education in the afternoons. "He's just attached a hitch to the bumper of his truck. To test tensile strength, the teacher links a boat trailer to his vehicle. The student is asked to drive it around the parking lot, the weld breaks, and the trailer falls off. Now do you think that the welding teacher is going to give your son an *A* because he spent *so much time* on the project?" The question hung in the air for about ten seconds. The mother looked confused and then desperately announced, "But studying the Bible should be different!"[364]

Though the mother's attitude would never be condoned by an athletic coach, educators put up with incessant parental and student whining. Unfortunately, culture has conditioned Christian thinking. Excuses unacceptable on the athletic field are condoned in the classroom, the physical trumping intellectual pursuit. Conditioning the interior life should be the same as physical conditioning. The opposite of whining in Christian academic rigor must be what biblical writers referred to as "inclining one's heart."[365] Athletes prepare hard: "There is no off season," goes the saying. "Suit up!" "Get your head in the game!" "Dedication," "commitment," and "all in" are statements adorning school practice jerseys. The same ideas reverberate through the First Testament phrase "incline your heart."

"Incline[366] your heart" means to bend, stretch, or extend—clear connections to the physical world. Like coaches, wise people were to be heard.[367] The figurative usage of the phrase can mean the negative—one has shifted his or her loyalty, apostatized, or been swayed.[368] Jeremiah constantly linked lack of listening and so obedience with "inclining their ear toward God."[369] The command is active and urgent: "Put away foreign gods and incline your heart to Yahweh, the God of Israel!"[370] But what strikes me in this study is the believers' *command to God to make us incline our ears*. Psalm 119:36 is one such case: "Incline my heart to your testimonies, and not unto profit-making."

Colin Duriez examines Francis Schaeffer's "crisis" as he reevaluated his whole Christian belief system in the early 1950s.[371] Schaeffer was driven in his spirit to reconsider his commitment. Having been convinced again of biblical assumptions and evidence, Schaeffer inclined his thinking and teaching toward Yahweh the rest of his life.

One of the most brilliant minds in Christ's church was Blaise Pascal. Pascal's passion for study wrote these words for every parent, all students, and me, who attempt to wriggle free from our true bent—proper inclination toward our Maker: "In short, we must resort to habit once the mind has seen where the truth lies ... it makes us believe things, and so inclines all our faculties to this belief that our soul naturally falls into it. When we believe only the strength of our conviction ... that is not enough. We must therefore make both parts of us believe: the mind by reasons ... and by habit, not allowing it any inclination to the contrary: *Incline my heart*."[372]

Why is it that we laugh at the mother who wants to give her child athlete a do-over? What we would never accept on the playing field, we fight for in the schoolroom. Some adults think that time spent and effort exerted should be standard enough for academics. A Christian view of study must take into account the One who made us, reminders of our responsibility in His Word, and our collective desire to find excuses for our lazy thinking. Leaning into our work—inclining our hearts—would be the proper response. Christian athletics and academics should have the same focus: development of the person's character through hard work.

Walking: If You Get Lost

Just because the road is well traveled does
not mean it is the right path.

You would think she carried the Holy Grail. That is how my friend treated the return of my season one *Lost* DVDs. First prompted by the nail-biting episodes, some formed groups that met to watch the program each week. My friends were playing catch-up. While most people will not be stranded on a desert island, many were drawn to the great questions the series raised, especially during its premier season. In an unusual way, *Lost* became found. People discovered directions for life.[373]

Getting lost or having the wrong directions could mean death in biblical times. The ease of online maps via Internet connections was nonexistent. Modern hotels did not exist. Fast food only applied to how quickly one walked and ate what he or she brought from home. The roads themselves were little more than well-worn footpaths. Apart from a few major trade routes, daily travel was quite limited. Robbers also made a journey perilous: witness Jesus' Good Samaritan story.[374] It was best to travel in caravans with others.[375]

While travel was much more treacherous in biblical times than today, knowing one's way—moving from lost to found—has always been crucial. A person could be on the way to the Red Sea or traversing the road back to Jerusalem from exile,[376] but most often, the words referred to one's course of life. Believers were to guard their ways so that they would not sin following directions contrary to "ways of darkness" and "crooked paths."[377] Ezekiel, for instance, consistently warned Israel that God would judge its ways, calling for its people to turn from their wicked direction.[378]

The idea of two ways was introduced in Deuteronomy.[379] One could choose life or death.[380] Yahweh, as Lord over Israel, stipulated that His people follow His way of life. Moses' fifth book was written in the form of a suzerain vassal treaty. The suzerain or king established rules of living for the vassal or servant in the ancient world. The pattern of responsibilities of Israel as the vassal to Yahweh, the suzerain, was established by the repetition of the phrase "walking in the ways" of the Lord.[381] The first time the phrase was used in Deuteronomy 5:33, the normal Hebrew word order (verb, subject, object) was reversed: "In all the ways which Yahweh your God has commanded you, you shall walk." The emphasis is placed on the path one follows.[382]

How one follows, noted by the Hebrew preposition "in," is important. "In" can express both the condition of something and its movement toward a goal.[383] "Walking in the ways of God" equally explains who I am and where I am going. I am both actively engaged in pursuing God's ways and participating in God's ways.[384] Notice the 360-degree evaluation. "Walking in God's ways" encompasses the person, her place, and the intention and objective of her action as well as her moment-by-moment response. In short, every aspect of a believer's life is governed by a heavenly GPS.[385]

A group coming to the retreat center where I was director got lost on the country roads at night. After multiple phone calls, I told them to stay where they were; I would find them and lead them back to our location. Sometimes directions are not enough to find our way. If we are lost, we want to be found.[386] The television series *Lost* taught us that we want answers to our questions—direction for life. But God does not simply give directions. He "goes after the one that is lost" until he or she is found[387] and then says, "Come, follow me."[388]

Walking: *With*-ness

Travel partners explain something of our destinations.

I scored 126th out of 126 students. When I was a junior in high school, our class took a test for possible college-level English curriculum in our senior year. Having been told the results, I sat sobbing on my bedroom floor. For some reason, grammatical prowess in my mother tongue eluded me. Syntax seemed like "sin tax" to me.

It was not until I learned another language that I began to understand my own. I fell in love with small words that told other words what to do and where to go. I was introduced to "from," "in," "through," and other prepositions in college Greek classes.[389] The importance of directional connectors cannot be overestimated. To this day, I am impressed by the versatility of language, the multicolored interaction of words with each other.

"With" is a key preposition when it comes to human interaction with God. *With* suggests relationship: closeness, proximity, interaction that is impossible apart from another.[390] From the earliest pages of Scripture, God desired long-term, continual, personal presence by walking *with* His people.[391] But Enoch and Noah are singled out as ones who "walked *with* God."[392] Choice between the paths of Abel[393] and Cain are clearly marked in Genesis 4. Abel's replacement, Seth, fathered Enoch, whose birth gave new hope for change. Not many people took the initiative to walk *with* God; in Genesis 5, Enoch and Noah set the standard.[394]

For Israel at large, God used the literary format of the day to communicate His clear instruction: "The least you can do as my servant nation is to follow me." The form of the book is organized around a suzerain-vassal treaty, which was a cultural agreement in that world. Victorious in battle, the king (suzerain) had the right to demand obedience from the servant (vassal) nation. God, the suzerain, expected Israel, the vassal, to obey Him. Meeting the baseline measure of God's expectation is to do as Deuteronomy 6:14 commands—not to "follow other gods" but only to "follow after God" (13:4). There seems to be a lowest possible denominator here that one would at least do this—give obedience to God and not other gods. Following God is a covenantal obligation. Loyalty is expected.[395]

Some are said to have "walked before" God.[396] David "followed after" God, as did Josiah.[397] While Israel is commended for following God in the desert in Jeremiah 2:2, only a few verses later, in Jeremiah 2:23, God said these same people ran after other gods. Yet there will come a day in the future Zechariah foretold when "Ten men from all languages and nations will take firm hold of one Jew by the edge of his robe and say, 'Let us go with you, because we have heard that God is *with* you.'"[398]

But covenantal people should walk *with* God.[399] The idea seems to be very specific, unusual, something not routine. Once in the Minor Prophets, God is said to be *with* His priest Zerubbabel, tying the covenant to His closeness with His servant.[400] But in Malachi 2:4–6, we learn of Levi the priest: "He walked *with* me in peace and uprightness, turning many from sin." There too, the covenant is mentioned. In Levi's case, the man took the initiative.

So what is my responsibility? It should come as no real surprise that Micah 6:8 is mentioned here: "And what does the Lord require of you? To act justly and to love mercy and to walk humbly *with* your God."

To walk *with* God seems to be quite different than following after or walking before Him. The preposition matters. A high benchmark is set. Walking *with* God means side by side, not behind or in front of. There is a sense of accompaniment, of *with*-ness possible between me and my Maker. Not only do I now understand the grammatical *with*-ness, but I also desire the intimacy of *with*-ness.

Walking: Don't Be Good for Goodness' Sake

How we walk tells where we go.

"Trim ten pounds for Christmas by walking," suggests an exercise headline. The Mayo Clinic advises walking for healthier lives.[401] Physical therapists tell us continual motion over years sustains long life.[402] There are websites for walkers where one can go to find any information necessary to begin or get better at walking.[403] And if you want the A to Z of hoofing it, read Geoff Nicholson's *The Lost Art of Walking: The History, Science, and Literature of Pedestrianism.*[404]

For my part, I have been walking for years. At present, my feet pound twenty-five miles of pavement each week. Folks wave to me as I traverse the road. Even the deer, rabbits, and birds stand and watch with interest—from a distance. While I know aerobic exercise has multiple benefits for my body, there is a constant struggle of commitment. Sometimes just getting out the door is a victory! In addition, devotion must be followed by repetition. Logging those miles necessitates a steady, step-by-step gait.

Consistency marked the Hebrews' use of the word for *walking.*[405] The idea behind treading the roads of one's time on earth was the metaphor of conduct, "the whole bent of the life."[406] The first two times Scripture uses the word, focus is on how humans lost their proper walk. The walkway to the garden was blocked, and their walking ways caused the flood.[407] Thereafter, Abram's line walked in a different direction, marching to a different drummer.[408] From this point on in Scripture and church history, when one walks, the pace of life is to be wholly dedicated to the Lord.[409]

The theme of walking is linked closely with wholeness. The imagery comes from shepherding: "If you want to become whole ... you must walk before me; you must place yourself under my exclusive supervision, guidance, and protection."[410] The "whole round of the activities of the individual life" is referenced continuously in the New Testament letters, especially those of Paul and John.[411] *Walk,* used as a code of conduct, was unique in the language of the day, making the Christian walk one of a kind.[412]

So when Paul compared a Christian's past life with his or her current lifestyle, the apostle said these are ways we formerly walked, we are no longer to walk this way.[413] Our habits change. Our lives are to be different from those of unbelievers. How? We are to walk in the Spirit. A short list includes being honest, truthful, loving, wise, orderly, obedient, and doing good works.[414] We are to walk in a way that is worthy of or pleasing to God. The word indicates that our actions are not simply outward displays of the Christmas carol, "Just be good for goodness' sake." Ours are not simple acts of service. Our reasons for walking down a certain road are our inner motives, totally given to Jesus, without thought of ourselves.[415]

James Houston's writing best describes the interiority of the Christian life. I have read and reread passages of his book *Joyful Exiles: Life in Christ on the Dangerous Edge of Things.* Houston explains how sin has so invaded our inner lives that, among other things, we believe being good for goodness' sake is what it means to be Christlike. Quoting Augustine, Houston concludes, "Where I am most inwardly myself, there You are far more than I."[416]

Before I walk in Christ according to Colossians 2:6, my inner being must bow to "this mystery, which is Christ in you, the hope of glory" (1:27). I am about to begin my exercise for the day—walking. With each footfall, I will contemplate yet again how my whole life can be unified for Christ, "being good for Jesus' sake."

Walking: Walk On

No one said this was going to be easy.

Putting one foot in front of the other is difficult some days. Robert Robinson was the eighteenth-century Cambridge pastor who penned the famous hymn, "Come, Thou Fount of Every Blessing." The positive nature of the song seemed not to reflect his hard later life. The story is told of his encounter one day with a woman who was studying a hymnal. She asked how he liked the hymn she was humming. In tears, Robinson replied, "Madam, I am the poor unhappy man who penned that tune many years ago, and I would give a thousand worlds, if I had them, to enjoy the feelings I had then."[417]

When I hear that story, I think of the phrase in Robinson's song, "Prone to wander, Lord I feel it / prone to leave the God I love." Another hymn writer, William Cowper, seems to have been cut from the same cloth. Depression dogged Cowper all his days. "God Moves in a Mysterious Way" is one of Cowper's songs. The phrase "Behind a frowning providence / he hides a smiling face" reflects, perhaps, the two-sided perspective of a man battling his own inner turmoil yet trusting the "fountain filled with blood, flowing from Emmanuel's veins"—the hymn for which Cowper is best known.[418]

Response to suffering and agony takes many forms. We feel what we feel intensely. We cry out with the Psalmist, as he did four times in a row, "How long, O Lord?"[419] The writer does not question God's intervention but His delay: "Why are you taking so long?" We suspect the loss of God's nearness. God has not left, but we do not sense the shine of His face on us any longer.[420]

"I have suffered much."[421] Let that statement hang in the air for a moment. There are those of us who feel that suffering every day—fingernails scraping across the blackboard of life. Screeching matches our latch on to the Psalms in our cries toward heaven. "I have suffered much" comes from

Psalm 119:105–113, capturing some of Robinson and Cowper's sentiments. While the source of suffering comes from without, this verse indicates an inner unrest: an affliction eating away at us that was caused by others.

Note the context. The previous verses suggest "evil" and "wrong paths."[422] Indeed, the wicked set snares on them.[423] Fighting internal turmoil because of external havoc, the writer says he takes his life in his own hands.[424] Earlier, he declared, "I am laid low in the dust" after "they almost wiped me from the earth."[425] Sometimes we face opposition, hatred, suppression, or oppression from others. Walking this life is hard.

So how do we make it down the road? The lamp that is our light from the famed Psalm 119:105 is not a general comment about Scripture's illumination. In my study, I have a set of lamp reproductions based on finds from various archaeological digs. All these lamps would fit in the palm of an adult human hand. The single wick gave off scant light—perhaps enough to see the next step or two on a moonless night. Sitting on a lamp stand, the candle-like quality could function as a night light for us, at best. In contrast, our twenty-first-century mind-sets think a lamp equals a halogen headlight, casting a beam hundreds of feet into the murky darkness. The Psalmist celebrates no such thing. All we have is a lamp that gives enough light for us to know the next step we take.[426]

Our lives' walks are based on Scriptural trust in things we cannot see.[427] If we are serious about walking down the path set by God, we must have no illusions about understanding why our present circumstances may be so hard. This section of Psalm 119[428] concludes with the writer saying he will follow God's Word "to the end." Until our missions on earth are complete, we continue walking with the light of Scripture that tells us only what we need to know.[429] In theological terms, the perseverance of the saints teaches in part that we bear the responsibility of obedience without expectation of certain outcomes.

Daw Aung San Suu Kyi is a Burmese activist who protested her government's treatment of its people. While marching with some of her supporters one day, soldiers blocked their path, leveling automatic weapons at the group. Suu Kyi kept walking despite orders to stop.[430] John Boorman made the woman's suffrage a focal point of his 1995 film *Beyond Rangoon*. The famed Irish rock band U2 created a title commemorating Suu Kyi's simple action: "Walk On." No phrase better represents Robinson's, Cowper's, Suu Kyi's, or my passage on earth in the midst of suffering than that we *walk on*.

Walking: He Went First

A guide is necessary when the path seems unseen.

Pioneers. Explorers. Trailblazers. Others have gone before us, and it's a good thing. Forerunners like Lewis and Clark established the possibilities of roads that moved people westward. Neal Armstrong will forever be remembered for his leap from the lunar space module. Rosa Parks has a name synonymous with standing up by sitting down. Vistas and horizons can be conquered because someone else traversed the land first.

God sets the pattern for all human activity, including the routine of walking. Indeed, the idea of the verb in Genesis 3:8 suggests that not only did God regularly move about in the garden He had made, but also that He did so for Himself.[431] Adam and Eve knew God's habit, being alerted by hearing His approaching footsteps.[432] God went traveling. He moved to and fro.[433]

What is the significance of such a cryptic statement as "God walked?" The personal God is invested, involved, connected; communion with humanity is His habit. The response of sinful men and women has been to stop walking, to hide. It was not until Enoch that humans could claim the same action—a continual traveling companion with God.[434] In order for us humans to reestablish walking as a God-given activity, we must reestablish our walks with God.[435]

The opposite of walking with God is to be directionless, meandering through life. Cain's line demonstrated the problem when one has no direction: we wander through life.[436] The alternative to a travel plan is to wander aimlessly. Being a vagabond is a homeless situation. One is without roots. Instability makes a person mentally unsteady, wavering, a reed swaying in the wind.[437] The opposite of walking is endlessly wandering. The endless end is endlessness.

But Leviticus 26:12, "I will walk among you," recaptures the original intention of God. Here the presence of God is said to be in His dwelling, His tabernacle with His people.[438] In fact, the reason God established a place to live with His people was so that God could move among them.[439] Walking in the garden and in the tabernacle both indicate God's presence with His people.

The tabernacle became flesh in the New Testament in the person of Jesus. God's movement amid humanity bears repeating: "The Word became flesh and tabernacled for a while among us."[440] In this way, Jesus is our forerunner, our pioneer, the One who has gone before us. He tasted death for everyone, sharing our humanness, preceding us into heaven.[441] Jesus is the source of salvation for all who obey Him, saving completely.[442] The earthly tabernacle was simply a copy of Him, the perfect tabernacle, who was sacrificed once to take away the sins of many people.[443]

Pioneers are not the only people who walk toward storied vistas. Walking with God is now possible again.

Path: The Path Runs through Me

Where I'm from can be a marker of where I'm going.

Country music is a combination of rock, folk, blues, and down-home, southern-style guitar strummin' that has captured my tapping toe. Sometimes I find myself catching up on recent top twenty videos from CMT or flipping the channel in my car to the local station to hear the latest from Sugarland, Brantley Gilbert, Jason Aldean, Miranda Lambert, or this one from Little Big Town:

> I feel no shame;
> I'm proud of where I came from.
> I was born and raised
> In the boondocks.
>
> One thing I know:
> No matter where I go,
> I keep my heart and soul
> In the boondocks.

When one listens to country music, there is a pride of country. You won't find patriotism in Hollywood, but you'll hear the stars and stripes wave in songs from Nashville. It is the tie to place, where one's from, that grabs my attention. Place gets into one's person. Hometown feels like down home. Locale is mental. The lyrics from "Boondocks" continue, "And I can feel that muddy water running through my veins." Where I'm from tells someone about who I am.

My identity (who I am) is marked by place (where I come from) and indicates my direction (how I get there). "Path" is not simply something I'm on, but what should be in me, what should run through me. My feet and heart are to walk on the same path.[444] Every wrong path can be understood by God's precepts within me.[445] God's Word is the light for how I think— my internal path.[446] I need to say with the Psalmist, "Direct me in the path of your commands, for there I find delight ... Turn my eyes away from worthless things, and renew my life in your way."[447] Path is a choice I make to live a certain way, and the way becomes my path.[448]

In *The Valley of Vision*, a collection of Puritan prayers, there is a canticle entitled "The Gospel Way." In part, it reads, "Blessed be thou, O Father, for contriving this way, Eternal thanks to thee, O Lamb of God, for opening this way, Praise everlasting to thee, O Holy Spirit, for applying this way to my heart. Glorious Trinity, impress the gospel on my soul, until its virtue diffuses every faculty; Let it be heard, acknowledged, professed, felt."[449] The gospel way should become my way, leading me down the way.

Where I'm from tells some about who I am. Where I walk infuses my thought and talk. The gospel way is my way. As the country runs through country music, so the path I'm on runs through me.

Path: *Quo Vadis?*

There is no middle way.

"Where are you going?" (Latin, *"Quo vadis?"*) is the famous phrase from the title of the novel by Polish Nobel Prize author Henryk Sienkiewicz. The book *Quo Vadis?* was made into multiple adaptations on the big screen. A Roman soldier in love with a Christian woman must come to understand why she believes as she does in the midst of Roman persecution. Peter's question of Jesus in John 13:36 began the discussion. The Latin question *"Quo vadis?"* is a query everyone must ask and answer as one considers where she or he is going in life.

How we get where we are going, what road we take, is essential. Life as a road has been a popular metaphor in literature, used in such famous works as *The Odyssey, The Aeneid, The Divine Comedy,* and *The Lord of the Rings.* Most recently, Cormac McCarthy *(No Country for Old Men)* penned an apocalyptic thriller simply titled *The Road.* McCarthy's view of life has limited hope. McCarthy's slight belief that someone will go ahead of us to keep the fire alive is small consolation for "the end of the road."

Songwriters have flirted with the picture of a road. Willie Nelson can't wait to get back "On the Road Again." By "rolling down the highway," Jim Croce hopes "life won't pass him by." Rascal Flatts remade the fist-pumping "Life Is a Highway" for a new generation of those who want to "ride it all night long." Even Carrie Underwood says, "Jesus, Take the Wheel" so she might be saved "from this road I'm on."

But how do we find the right road to get us where we need to go? Psalm 17:5 declares, "My steps have held to your paths." The Lord says in Jeremiah 6:16, "Stand at the crossroads and look; ask for the ancient paths, ask where the good way is, and walk in it, and you will find rest for your souls."[450] God's way, or course of living, is found in His commandments.[451] "Walk in all the way that the Lord your God has commanded you" is a repetitious theme throughout Scripture.[452]

Some declare they have stayed on the path, while others ask to be shown the road.[453] Ultimately, there is a choice to be made. There is a good way, "the way of the Lord," or the evil way that travels in the opposite direction.[454] Some follow "the way of Balaam" or heretics who walk in the "way of Cain."[455] But Peter refers to Christianity as "the way of truth," "the right way," and "the way of righteousness."[456] And God knows every person's path.[457]

Perhaps *"Quo vadis?"* can be answered with a heavenly GPS (global positioning system). Jesus' sacrifice opened a "new and living way," since He is "the way."[458] For the Roman soldier, Peter, and all of us, the answer to the question is the same: Jesus.

Next, the question "Where are you going?" demands another: "How do you get there?" Eugene Peterson reminds us that the how is desperately important:

> I want to counter the common reduction of "way" to a road, a route, a line on a map—a line that we can use to find our way to eternal life; such reduction means the elimination of way as a metaphor, the reduction of way to a lifeless technology. The Way that is Jesus is ... the way he acted, felt, talked, gestured, prayed, healed, taught, and died. And the way of his resurrection. The Way that is Jesus cannot be reduced to information or instruction. The Way is a person whom we believe and follow as God-with-us.[459]

Genesis 4 opens history's map to two roads. The road of Cain leads to rebellion, the road of Abel to righteousness. There are only two choices; there is no middle road. In the American South, folks would say, "You're either for Him or agin' Him." Jesus said there are two paths. One is wide and easy, leading to destruction; the other is narrow and hard, leading to life. Jesus' way is the ancient path, the road less taken, the way to life, the way of life.

Path: A Pilgrimage

No one wants to be on the wrong path.

W hen I was a boy, my teachers taped cardboard cutouts of a Thanksgiving scene to the classroom windows. Indians were always seen harvesting corn, the women were always setting a table, and the men always had a musket in one hand and a dead turkey in the other. The holiday was whitewashed a bit from the original scene.

We were not privy to the horrendous living conditions. We were not told that half the inhabitants died that first winter. The Thanksgiving holiday,[460] wholly passed over in our rush to Christmas consumption, was in part to remember these hearty souls, anxious for religious freedom at great physical cost.[461] Pilgrims, a term first used by William Bradford, governor of Plymouth Colony, was given to the first group of Christian separatists traveling on *The Mayflower,* coming from religious persecution in England.[462]

Pilgrims, whether disenfranchised believers seeking freedom from religious tyranny or displaced from their original homeland, have never walked an easy path. The word "pilgrimage" gives us the idea of a sojourn or residency in a land not one's own.[463] A pilgrim is what Scripture calls an alien or a stranger.[464] For the original American Pilgrims, the concept of covenant, the need to work together for the good of all, was essential for their future longevity.[465]

The Pilgrim's Progress captures the essence of Christian pilgrimage. No other book, apart from the Bible, has been so continuously published and read as John Bunyan's classic. Bunyan's early life was volatile and vile. But his autobiographical *Grace Abounding to the Chief of Sinners* states Bunyan was rescued by Jesus. The line that haunts Christian, and so each Christian, is stated by Evangelist: "Your sin is very great. It involves two evils: you forsook the right way, and you walked in a forbidden path." No one wants to be on the wrong path.

The Song of Ascents (Psalms 120–134) reminds the believer that there is one road, that the pilgrimage is toward one place for one reason. These Psalms were chanted or sung by religious pilgrims as they made their way up to Jerusalem (or Zion) to celebrate Levitical festivals three times a year.[466] In the Old Testament economy, getting from place to place was a highway formed by people "treading or trampling" a path worn by constant walking.[467] People were on the way to someplace to complete a mission[468].

The pilgrimage took great effort for one purpose. Walter Brueggemann, in his pioneering book *The Land: Place as Gift, Promise, and Challenge in Biblical Faith,* says, "Place is space that has historical meanings, where some things have happened that are now remembered and that provide continuity and identity across generations. Place is space in which important words have been spoken that have established identity, defined vocation, and envisioned destiny. [So] a yearning for a place is a decision to enter history with an identifiable people in an identifiable pilgrimage."[469]

The Pilgrims who landed at Plymouth on Cape Cod were no different than Old Testament pilgrims visiting Jerusalem. Each group of believers was dedicated to a way of life. As *The Pilgrim's Progress* reminds us still, this sojourn is not easy. But Christians are pilgrims together. We walk the path holding hands with others in both celebration and lamentation. We are from another place, but we are in this place for this time. Perhaps the day will come when a teacher somewhere tapes cutouts of us on a classroom window. Can't you hear it now? "Children, these were the twenty-first-century pilgrims."

Path: *Status Viator*

"We are on our way" takes on new significance.

"Life is a journey" has become a common phrase in the West. In the present culture, it seems it is the trip taken, not the destination that matters. Many, including Christians, blithely ask each other about their spiritual journeys without considering the source of the term or its general implications in society. According to some Eastern religious views, life is not about ends but about process. The idea is not so much that one is on the way to somewhere but simply out and about. Story, character, and relationship are artificially separated from conclusion, destination, and truth.

Hindu beliefs, for instance, claim the soul is on a cosmic journey to purify itself as it is reincarnated in other bodies.[470] One can purchase a "Life is a Journey" clock that "Reminds us that every path in life is a part of the journey. The destination is not the goal; it is making the trip."[471]

Anime[472] creators had a discussion this month comparing the concepts of journey versus destination. One cartoonist is "convinced that storytelling's a matter of preparation *and* resolution; 'getting there' might be diverting, but there ought to be a 'there' to get to and I'm not happy if I'm asked to supply the 'there' myself."[473]

Scripture sets the standard for destination. There are paths of uprightness,[474] justice,[475] and life.[476] Individuals are also given paths: Jeroboam, Ahab, Balaam, David, and Paul.[477] Clear teachings in both testaments establish an eternal end for believers and nonbelievers from Job[478] to David[479] to Malachi.[480]

History, intentionality, identity, and consummation must form the framework for our paths toward Christian residence with Jesus.[481] Jesus, whose constant linkage with the Old Testament established the historic roots of the Christian message, said that He himself is "from the Father," laying out His eternal history.[482] Our Lord's strict teaching about a "narrow path" demands designation, not wandering, as our goal in life.[483] Our identity with Christ is clear.[484] And Jesus' teaching about ends (e.g., heaven and hell) is more than any other speaker in the New Testament.

So what does this teaching about the Christian path mean for everyday life? Jesus is the way, the path that leads to life.[485] There is only one road on which one's end is eternal life. Life is not about finding oneself on some nebulous search. A journey for the Christian always has a final outcome, a goal, an end, a destination. Believers should be careful in using seemingly benign terminology to express how we live. Because of Providence, our plans, our ways, are ordered by heaven.[486] We should revisit the straightforward and famous injunction from Proverbs 3:6: "In all your ways acknowledge Him, and He will make your paths straight."

Alan Jacobs, quoting Joseph Pieper, writes,

> The concept of the *status viatoris* is one of the basic concepts of every Christian rule of life. To be a "viator" means "one on the way." The *status viatoris* is, then, the "condition or state of being on the way." Its proper antonym is *status comprehensoris*. One who has comprehended, encompassed, arrived, is no longer a *viator*, but a *comprehensor*.
>
> If we Christians can learn to think of our lives as ... stories that move along recognizable paths, paths followed by our predecessors and indeed by our contemporary companions in the faith—we will be better prepared for the *status viator*, better protected from the twin dangers of presumption and despair, better able to see changes in the road as continuations of it rather than detours from it or dead ends.[487]

A Christian's life is one of being on the way given by one guide with clearly marked, true directions on a specific highway leading toward a final destination.

Path: The Way

Finding one's way supposes one exists.

In 1929, the US Naval Academy unveiled a monument to Matthew Maury with the engraving "Pathfinder of the Seas." While others had discovered ocean currents prior to Maury's birth, Maury himself invested his life in helping mariners navigate the oceans' unseen streams. It is the phrase in Psalm 8:8, "All that swim in the paths of the seas," that may have led to Maury's being noted as the founder of modern oceanography.

For ages, explorers such as Columbus or Magellan sought to give humanity a way to traverse the oceans. The circumnavigation of the globe by Ferdinand Magellan sets the standard for such discoveries. The Straits of Magellan south of Chile, given for his accomplishments, expanded human knowledge by a means unknown in the sixteenth century. Using water routes with Magellan or land routes with Lewis and Clark, people seem intent on finding their way.

Continuing down the road of human discovery is an ongoing, never-ending process.[488] What we understand about the world may grow, but we have only scratched the surface.[489] Indeed, the Creator alone knows the way to wisdom.[490] Military triumph, unseen by the enemy, was had because He "made a way through the sea."[491] And while we enjoy the benefits of light and darkness, humans do not know their "places" or the "paths to their dwellings."[492]

But what happens when the Almighty Himself blocks "my way so I cannot pass ... shroud[ing] my paths in darkness"?[493] Why does God permit my enemies to "break up my road," allowing them to destroy me?[494] Even when He "knows my way," it seems it is still to take me intentionally down "the path I walk" where "men have hidden a snare for me."[495] At times, it is

my own sin for which He "drives me away, making me walk in darkness …
making my paths crooked."[496] Still, when I "have kept my feet from every
evil path," even my so-called friends "turn aside from their routes."[497]

Let's face it: we don't like the way of God—"my ways are not your
ways."[498] In all honesty, I struggle with "not my will but yours be done"[499] in
my Christ-unlike-ness. Outside of forgiving my enemies in the Lord's Prayer,
the hardest phrase for me to repeat (and mean!) is "your will be done on
earth."[500] I want the "level path."[501]

Leveling and straightening the road in preparation for a highway is
exactly the prophecy of what John the Baptist would do for Jesus.[502] But this
was no easy street! Temptation to crucifixion was a difficult traverse for the
Son of Man, and it would be no different for His followers. Matthew 7:13–14
says the path is narrow, and only a few find it. Victor Hamilton's work on
the Hebrew word for "way" reminds us, "Our Lord's reference to himself as
'the way, the truth, the life' means that Jesus is the way to the truth about
life. He is not the answer. That would be an oversimplification. He is the
way that leads to the answer."[503]

At times, we are left so far off the beaten track of life that we do not even
know what the question is, and now we are told there is no answer yet. We
are expected to be on the way, blind, walking unfamiliar paths, yet where
the rough places are made smooth.[504] It is no mistake that early Christians
called their belief "the way."[505] There is a clear road (Jesus), a clear path to
follow (Scripture), and a clear destination (heaven). What remains *unclear*
are the broken pavement, detours, and lane closures that make our ways
quite uncomfortable. To the One who placed paths in the seas that humans
trust for trade and travel, all I can do is trust "*You* (emphatic in Hebrew) who
know my way."[506]

Place: Thin Places

Christian study must begin by acknowledging another world.

Celtic Christianity teaches that there are "thin places"—locations where supernatural and natural worlds almost intersect spatially.[507] Sensitive folk have a sixth sense. Perhaps Elizabeth Barrett Browning's lines from "Aurora Leigh" capture the concept best with her line, "Earth's crammed with heaven, and every common bush afire with God: but only he who sees, takes off his shoes—the rest sit around and pluck blackberries."[508]

Church history is full of characters whose lives were intimately acquainted with supernatural sensitivities. Aidan of Lindisfarne brought the gospel to England after others declared the angles to be uncivilized.[509] It is Aidan's prayer that should focus our mission:

> Leave me alone with God as much as may be.
> As the tide draws the waters close in upon the shore,
> Make me an island, set apart,
> alone with you, God, holy to you.
> Then with the turning of the tide
> prepare me to carry your presence to the busy world beyond,
> the world that rushes in on me
> till the waters come again and fold me back to you.[510]

Brendan the Navigator established monasteries that functioned as places of contemplation as well as education.[511] St. Patrick prayed at day's beginning for God's "Host to save me from snares of demons ... I summon today all these powers between me and those evils, against ... incantations ... black

120

laws ... crafts of idolatry ... spells of witches and smiths and wizards ... every knowledge that corrupts man's body and soul."[512]

Historical, Scriptural events evidence the intersection of heaven and earth. Abraham entertained heaven in human form outside his tent in Genesis 18. Elisha asked Yahweh to open his servant's eyes to see the angelic army surrounding the physical Syrian army in 2 Kings 6. Supernatural battles keeping God's messengers from delivering a message were recorded in Daniel 10. Philip's inexplicable transfer from one location to another for evangelism is found in Acts 8. And Satan's contention for Moses' body with the archangel Michael was used as an example of worlds colliding in Jude 9.

A number of movies reflect a paranormal point of view. In *In the Electric Mist,* Tommy Lee Jones' character continues to meet a long-dead Civil War Confederate general who teaches him life lessons. *First Snow* presents a normal, everyday event transforming Guy Pearce, whose life is changed because of a predictive utterance given by a sideshow card-reader. *Seraphim Falls,* starring Liam Neeson and Pierce Brosnan, displays the awful consequences of the Civil War that so haunt the two characters that their lives become interpretations of desert prophets. *The Exorcism of Emily Rose* is an example of the horror genre, which acknowledges another world. Intersection of physic and mystic is a truer definition of reality.

The realism of Genesis 1:2, I believe, is the origin of thin places. The phrase "without form and void" is not chaos but the preordered world gently protected by the Spirit of God. Before structures and systems were established within creation, the raw materials were brought into being out of nothing. Supernatural Spirit protection incubated the preformed created elements as a mother bird incubates her eggs.[513] Unlike nonhistorical myths of the day, Genesis' primordial materials were not menacing, sinister, or chaotic.[514] God's personal presence in His world, the intersection of spirit and matter, began in Genesis 1:2. "The account leaves mysterious what cannot help but be mysterious."[515] As George MacDonald was heard to say over a century ago, "Whenever you begin to speak of anything true, divine, heavenly, or supernatural, you cannot speak of it at all without speaking about it wrongly in some measure. We have no words, we have no phrases, we have no possible combination of sentences that do more than represent fragmentarily the greatness of the things that belong to the very vital being of our nature."[516]

Our nature is a cohesive whole, the intersection of supernatural with natural. Living, including a commitment to study, is a mind committed to the things of the Spirit.[517] As we ponder the Creator's creation, a Celtic benediction "The Hermit's Song" could offer help toward an explanation of thin places.

> I wish, O Son of the living God, O ancient, eternal King
>
> For a hidden little hut in the wilderness, That it may be my dwelling ...
>
> Quite near, a beautiful wood, Around it on every side
> To nurse many-voiced birds, Hiding it with its shelter ...
>
> Raiment and food enough for me, From the King of fair fame
> And I to be sitting for a while, Praying God in every place.
>
> In the infinity of night skies, in the free flashing of lightening, in whirling elemental winds, you are God. In the impenetrable mists of dark clouds, in the wild gusts of lashing rain, in the ageless rocks of the sea, you are God and I bless you. You are in all things and contained by no thing. You are the Life of all life and beyond every name. You are God and in the eternal mystery I praise you.

Place: Rootedness in the Sacred

The act of creation needs incarnation for our best contemplation.

"We live in virtual relationships," Kaycee explained.

Russ added, "We serve Facebook rather than allowing Facebook to serve us."

"We only have so much time," Katie rightly ascertained, "only so much emotion to give. Can we continue far-flung relationships with those whom we no longer live with?"

The conversation continued in rapid fashion. The discussion parsed word choices and exegeted others' comments, making sure of what they heard. But I was struck by my students' acknowledgment, the unstated need, for relationship in proximity. How much do we have need for longevity in a place to build physical, visible relations with others? How necessary is the day-in-day-out connection with folks who know us best in all our moods, situations, or interactions?

Our discussion concerned Sertillanges' book *The Intellectual Life*,[518] which remarked on organizing one's life, commenting, "Avoid, even with these, the excessive familiarity which drags one down and away from one's purpose; do not run after news that occupies the mind to no purpose; do not busy yourself with the sayings and doings of the world, that is with such as have no moral or intellectual bearing; avoid useless comings and goings which waste hours and fill the mind with wandering thoughts."

The intentional choice to live a long time in one place cements "the first association of the intellectual ... with his fellows."[519] We may think alone, but we must think together. Mobile Americans, however, do not establish roots in communities. As the *Indianapolis Star* reported,

While promotions or new, better-paying jobs typically mean new wealth, the increasingly rootless habits of Americans has come at a price, leading to declining participation in neighborhood organizations and local politics and frayed connections to the community at large. "The overall impetus in society is towards mobility, of searching for prosperity," said Scott Russell Sanders, author of the book *Staying Put: Making a Home in a Restless World*. "(But) we are so enamored of mobility that we don't recognize what is being lost in the process.[520]

Place is necessary. Michael Pollan, in his book *A Place of My Own*,[521] declares that ground is sacred, that each of us looks for a privileged place that is invested with meaning. Sacred places began with "the heavens and the earth."[522] Yahweh gave land to Israel, "a land flowing with milk and honey," where boundary stones would secure Israelites "a place of [their] own."[523] In an early response to care of creation, heaven's injunction included, "Are the trees of the field people that you should besiege them?"[524] One of Judah's great kings, Uzziah, was said to have "loved the soil."[525] When God's original intention is restored, "every man will sit under his own fig tree," culminating in "the New Heavens and Earth."[526]

God's original intention for humans was a linkage to their origin, the ground. We are never to forget where we came from, where we're going, and for what we are responsible. We are rooted to the ground. We have a place and know our place. We invest in our place. Place is property and ownership. Place demands a boundary. Place identifies individuality and nationality. Place must be protected. Place can be holy or a memorial. Without a place, we are lost, nomads, refugees—people without a country. Communities spring up because there is a common commitment to place by the people who live there.

Any permanence that can be acknowledged in this life is tied to the ground on which we walk, the property we own. The pieces of land we call our own will survive us—we who have but seventy to eighty years of life to live. It would seem clear that our best efforts on this earth and in this life should focus on loving our neighbors by creating from our places so that provisions of food and shelter would be abundant. We must prepare our places for the next generation and the next generation for our places.

Preparing the next generation includes a place to study where people join in community learning.

My students' concern about enjoying relationships and learning in a place questions the virtual, technological world they know. The necessity of rootedness continues to be necessary for us all to have our places. From Genesis to Revelation, it seems God's intention is not so much for electrons and mobility but for the consistent universal cry for a place to call our own.

Place: There Is No "There" There

Learning is accomplished within a person, in a place, with people.

"There is no 'there' there" famously wrote Gertrude Stein in *Everybody's Autobiography*. Gone from her hometown of Oakland for some time, she returned, looking for her childhood home. The house was not there: Stein's "there" was nowhere to be found. Mark Edmundson used Stein's quote to highlight the vulnerability of his college students:

> At a student party, about a fourth of the people have their cellphones locked to their ears. What are they doing? "They're talking to their friends." About? "About another party they might conceivably go to." And naturally the simulation party is better than the one that they're now at (and not at), though of course there will be people at that party on their cellphones, talking about other simulacrum gatherings, spiraling on into M. C. Escher infinity.[527]

During a class one day, Edmundson took a poll. He asked his students, "How many places were you simultaneously yesterday—at the most?" Between cells, texts, Macs, iPods, books, and an occasional glance at the teacher, some surpassed the level of ten. Edmundson concludes, "Be everywhere now—that's what the current technology invites, and that's what my students aspire to do."

I was invited to be a consultant for a Christian college. My task was to listen and be an outside voice responding to what I saw in a day dedicated to training student leaders. I am concerned about life's distractions, a product of dichotomy, division, and disassociation rooted in the effects of Genesis 3.

I suggested to the group that unity is the essence of community—functioning with one voice in one direction on one mission. Distraction and fragmentation, both results of sin, force our minds in too many directions, mandate that we do too many things and belong to too many organizations. The myth of multitasking, born of our humanistic tendency toward omniscience and omnipresence, emphasizes diversity over unity, individuality over community. The Hebraic concepts of *shalom* (peace, wholeness, fulfillment) and *sabbat* (rest) suggest that our finite, fallen selves should focus on a few things instead of many things.

Our desire for more points toward our true interest. Simply put: we want to be God. Our puny attempt to usurp heaven's throne was a grasping for authority not our own. We want to be all things to all people. We want to control all situations. We want to be everywhere at once. We want, we want, we want. The prefix "omni-" suggests "every" and "all," the same spirit found in Edmundson's students—the same spirit found in us all.

Is there a solution to our pompous belief that "every" and "all" belong to us? What is the response to a world that desires to be everywhere but finds there is no "there" there? Humans are tied to one place at one time, whether we like it or not. Electron feeds are not atomic feet—flesh and bone are resident here at this moment in time as I sit in my chair. Peggy Noonan rightly complained to journalist friend who is a podcaster "that he seems to be speaking from No Place."[528]

Ray Oldenbury encourages us to find *The Great Good Place: Cafes, Coffee Shops, Bookstores, Bars, Hair Salons, and Other Hangouts at the Heart of a Community*. Movies such as *Places in the Heart, The River, Fried Green Tomatoes,* or *The Field* might offer visual examples of people who care deeply enough for place that they will invest their lives for it. In the educational world, Suzanne Kelly is correct that institutional foci and loci must be on "the embodiment of learning."[529] Arthur W. Hunt III, writing on Internet universities and flesh-and-blood teachers, summarizes, "We should not deceive ourselves into believing that an online education is on a par with real-presence learning. In the rush to digitize the college classroom, we should remember the sheer power of embodied teaching—that real love is transmitted through real presence."[530]

Presence in a place necessitates a theology of place. Connection to people and place has its origins in Genesis. God uses wordplay in Genesis 1–3 to suggest the importance of the connection between *adam* (man) and *adamah* (ground). I intentionally leave the verses in the text to show how much the words connect.

We are tied directly to the ground. God created ground (Genesis 1:10), establishing the physical basis upon which creatures would live life (1:25). The ground belonged to God, which He sustained with water (2:3–6). Humanity was brought from the ground to work the ground (2:5). The ground would then produce food for human sustenance and pleasure (2:9). In addition, animals were molded from the ground (2:19), creating obvious similarities and differences with people.

After sin, maintenance of the ground (2:15) brought with it hardship (3:17) and relocation for production (3:23). Before sin, humans brought fruit up from the ground (2:5, 9). After sin, people would go down to the ground (3:19). However, while the ground was cursed, humanity was not (3:17). Crops from the ground were to be given as a physical display of thanks to the One who gave it (4:2–3). However, the best—not the leftovers—was intended. The ground even allowed shed blood to bear witness of crime (4:10–11) while its productivity was withheld as a punishment for the criminal (4:11–12, 14).

The curse of the ground by God was not left without its comfort or rest brought by Noah, whose name means just that—"rest" (Genesis 5:29). The destruction of the ground (7:23) would not be done again (8:21). Even Noah is called "a man of the ground" (9:20). And from this lineage would come Abram, through whom "all peoples of the ground would be blessed" (Genesis 12:3).

Everything from geography to property rights to where one calls home is rooted in all people. This is because God has set the time and place for all people to live (Acts 17:26). I believe disjointedness is evidenced in our electronic world. A result of Genesis 3, rootlessness can be overcome by rootedness, the intention of Genesis 1.

Place: A Piece of Land to Call Our Own

Home gives us a place to study.

Does one's identity depend upon a cause and ultimately, a place? George Eliot examines this among other themes in her book *Daniel Deronda*. In an oft-quoted line (included, for example, as the opening frame to the movie *Gods and Generals*), she presses the issue of identity and place:

> A human life, I think, should be well rooted in some spot of a native land, where it may get the love of tender kinship for the face of earth, for the labours men go forth to, for the sounds and accents that haunt it, for whatever will give that early home a familiar unmistakable difference amidst the future widening of knowledge: a spot where the definiteness of early memories may be inwrought with affection, and kindly acquaintance with all neighbours, even to the dogs and donkeys, may spread not by sentimental effort and reflection, but as a sweet habit of the blood ... The best introduction to astronomy is to think of the nightly heavens as a little lot of stars belonging to one's own homestead.[531]

John Milton called it *Paradise Lost*—being displaced from our place in the Garden of Eden. What was lost, however, will be regained, the ground retained.[532] Not only will believers be fully restored to their original state as Adam, but the ground ("adamah") will also be returned as "the garden of Eden."[533]

From Genesis 2, we have been rooted to the ground. Owning a piece of ground produces thoughtful reflection. All people should be reminded of where they came from (the ground) and where they are going to (the ground). We are participants with God in managing the creation. Having a home is important to everyone. Community necessitates a place. To enable its members to be in community with others, the church must know its place—its setting, neighbors, culture, and locale. For the believer, "this world is my home, I'm not just passin' through," contrary to the gospel tune.

Established documents at the local church Zionsville Fellowship in Zionsville, Indiana explain the concept under the heading "The Church as a Community." "Community, if it is practical, implies geographical closeness ... Be careful about moving frequently. Mobility can be destructive to community. It has been easy for Christians to fall into the patterns of our secular world, which has little regard for community or continuity. Present relationships are often sacrificed for another job, house, or new pleasure."[534]

When I sit outside on a clear night, it is as if God has laid out a blanket of stars on black linen. I have often thought of Eliot's comment while there. I think about my place on this earth. I am grateful for worldwide beauty. I cherish my country, the United States of America. I enjoy all the wonders in the great state of Indiana. And I am a homebody—if I have a choice to go somewhere or stay in my own backyard, the car stays in the garage.

Yet there is restlessness in me for "the new heavens and new earth."[535] One of my professors in grad school told of his great longing to set up a bait shop at the southern tip of the Dead Sea when Jesus' return would let fresh water flow through it.[536] During the millennial kingdom, maybe I can visit Dr. Knife at his bait shop, and he can come for a visit to Indiana.

Place: Road Maps as Places in the Heart

We may walk on a property, but often the property walks through us.

M aps: Finding Our Place in this World[537] tells the story of life and lives through cartography (the study of maps). A companion volume to a Chicago Field Museum exhibit, *Maps* chronicles that geography is more than simply the lay of the land. An atlas charts not simply the place people live but how that place changes people.

It seems obvious from Genesis 10 that where a person lives impacts what he does and how he lives. We all come from common stock: all people everywhere are equal, since we are all blood.[538] Yet the Table of Nations genealogy emphasizes the connection land has to people. Land contributes to vocations:[539] where one lives may determine what he or she will do in life (e.g., living near water may indicate a maritime career). Land creates nations:[540] clans, nations, languages, and territories indicate sovereignty of what belongs to whom. Land creates home:[541] God set places for all to live.

Perhaps a map tells us as much about us as it does about our locations. People's lives can be shaped by places. Rob and Deb Wingerter are two such examples. The Wingerters are the patrons of Mahseh Center in north-central Indiana. Rob's vision for a retreat and study center began over twenty years ago on Lake Bruce. Deb's family roots there go back seventy years, allowing Mahseh to become reality. Here is the story, in Deb's own words. Hers is the link between people and place, between road maps and places in the heart.

> On April 17, 2007, my mother, Dortha Strong Waidner, left this world and joined Jesus in heaven. She was ninety-one years old and had lived a long and full life. She first came

to Lake Bruce in the 1930s because her grandfather, John Morton Strong, had a trailer on Guise Park Road. He didn't own land there, but he did some work for the Guises, and so they let him park his trailer there. In 1941, my grandfather, Clarence Strong, purchased five lots from Linc Overmeyer with the intention of building a cabin for his father. Clarence also wanted a place to come and fish and relax at the end of his work week at Studebakers in South Bend. The war came along, my uncles were drafted, and the cabin was not built until 1946. During construction, John Morton Strong died. So the cabin was used by all the Strongs and their church friends for resting and fishing.

In 1947, Dortha returned from living in California, and Lake Bruce became her refuge, a place of peace and renewal. In June of 1955, when I was eight months old, my mother packed up me, my older sister, and my nephew Billy, and my dad drove us to Lake Bruce. We stayed there all summer and early fall. My dad came on the weekends, and my mother and sister had no car during the week. When groceries were needed or ice for the icebox, my sister would row the fishing boat across the lake to Johnny Dillinger's store. They had no indoor plumbing, washed the diapers by hand, and hung them on the line to dry. But once again, Lake Bruce was my mother's refuge, a place for healing and hope.

Over the years, my mother and father developed many close friendships at Lake Bruce. May Kline, who lived in the house (now gone) at the corner of Lake Shore Drive and 150N, was a close friend of my mother's and my grandmother's. It was May's father, Linc, who had owned all the land on the east shore. Bill and Margaret Werner, who lived in the old Lake Bruce Hotel next to the railroad tracks (now gone), were also good friends. Margaret knew everything that went on at Lake Bruce, and anything you told her would most likely end up in the *Observer*, where Bill worked.

Lake Bruce has always been a special place created by God for people to come to for refuge and retreat. The peace and tranquility that comes with God's presence is there for all who come and open their hearts to it. For sixty-one years, it was my mother's refuge. Now she is where there is no need for refuge. Heaven, where there are no tears, no sorrow, no pain, is her home now. She was welcomed by my father, my sister, my grandparents, Bill and Margaret, May, and many, many others. I am so thankful that God has given me and my family this refuge to keep us going in this broken world until He calls us home.

The Wingerters share their place as a refuge for study and retreat. Place has certainly marked the Wingerter family. Often, we discover that where we live makes a difference in how we live. Neighbors, jobs, recreation, and landmarks impact who we are and what we become. Place matters. Maps can tell us where we live, but where we live often maps us.

Conclusion

In *The Island of Lost Maps*, Miles Harvey asks why the sense of discovery seemed to play such an important role for the [map] collector. During an interview with Werner Muensterberger, a psychology expert and author of *Collecting: An Unruly Passion*, Harvey explored the explorer's mind: "'Think of the word: dis-cover—to take the cover off and see what's there,' Muensterberger began. 'It goes very deep for the collector: I want to find out. And what you really want to find is, Where do I come from? What is the source? That is discovery—finding something no one knew before, and you didn't know before.'"[542]

Discovery has much the same sense as revelation: to uncover or disclose for the purpose of further understanding.[543] Earthly penchant for learning new things comes from heaven: "It is the glory of God to conceal things but the glory of kings is to search things out."[544] Kings in the ancient world were considered similar to a twenty-first-century patron of arts and sciences.[545] State sovereigns' pursuit of new intellectual thought was to bring honor to the universal Sovereign. As God has revealed Himself in His creation, so humans discover the creation the Creator has revealed.

Consequently, I am perplexed when I read that someone keeps his or her knowledge a secret from the rest of us. Online advertisements, for instance, entice the viewer to consider how someone lost forty-seven pounds because the person followed "this one secret." Of course, the draw is to get a person interested in the purchase of a product. The secret can be bought and sold. Dan Brown's *The Da Vinci Code* made Gnostic[546] secrets famous. During the first century, the church was besieged by people who believed they had special knowledge. Indeed, if you wanted the secret to life, you had to join their sect. Knowing Gnostic secrets meant payment was due in some form.

John and Paul smashed the pomposity of Gnostic heresies in their books of 1 John[547] and Colossians. It is Paul's phrase in Colossians 2:3 in particular that lampoons belief in secret information: "in whom [Christ] are hidden all the treasures of wisdom and knowledge."[548] Paul's admonitions hold at least four truths that all believers should apply to the Christian concept of study.

First, Christ is the storehouse of knowledge (hidden treasures). Christ is the layaway for the world's information and its application: it is laid up, treasured, stored away.[549] Paul used the Greek word that we still use today: *thesaurus*. A storehouse of words now was a storehouse of valuables then.[550] Jesus said a person focuses his or her attention on values he or she thinks are important, made obvious by life choices.[551] Proverbs 20:15 indicates that while financial riches exist, "the lips of knowledge are a precious jewel." Accumulation of heaven's wealth means a bank account focused on heaven's view of mental health.

Second, Christ's knowledge is exclusive ("in whom"). "In" in Greek can tell both the location and instrumentation of a subject.[552] So there are no brute facts. Neutrality is a myth. Equality of beliefs is impossible. A Christian view of study is broadminded in the sense that everything is open for investigation. A Christian, however, is close-minded (as is everyone to his or her own beliefs) in this: all knowledge is from and through Christ. John W. Peterson's hymn "A Student's Prayer" ties application to instruction:

May the things we learn, so meager, never lift our hearts in pride
Till in foolish self-reliance we would wander from Thy side.
Let them only bind us closer, Lord, to Thee, in whom we find
Very fountainhead of Wisdom, Light and life of all mankind.

Third, Christ is the source of knowledge ("wisdom and knowledge"). In Greek thought, knowledge came through the senses, and wisdom was equivalent to philosophical speculation.[553] Paul's use of the terms is exactly opposite. Hebrews personalized the heavenly origin of knowledge in wise living. The believer listens to the personification of Wisdom in Proverbs 8:34 as she says, "Blessed is the one who listens to me, watching daily at my gates, waiting beside my doors."

Arthur Holmes links a Christian view of study with similar themes that shaped St. Bonaventure's approach to learning: "Wisdom is written everywhere, Bonaventure insists, and the world is like a book written front and back, or a mirror imaging the presence of God in its order and beauty and light ... God's goodness emanates like a light diffusing itself throughout the entire creation; he is the exemplar, the Logos of all created things, and he is the one to whom it leads and for whom it all exists."[554]

Finally, Christ's control of knowledge is universal ("all"). As I often tell my students, "All means all, and that's all *all* means." Abraham Kuyper's oft-quoted sentence is clear: "there is not one square inch of earth over which Christ does not declare 'I am Lord!'"[555] Erasmus made his point earlier in church history: "All studies, philosophy, rhetoric are followed for this one object, that we may know Christ and honor him. This is the end of all learning and eloquence."[556] Human attempts either to fathom or discover more of Christ's knowledge—even of their physical realm—"are but the outer fringe of his works."[557]

I Just Need Time to Think! Reflective Study as Christian Practice is an encouragement to Christ-followers everywhere that we should honor Christ with our learning. Study should not be separated from our need to retreat. Discipline in education at times necessitates holiday to make it happen. Reading demands our reflection. Obstacles to study mean we need to keep on walking toward that goal. Our path of learning means that a place to study is indispensable. Each of fifty essays orbits around the theme that taking time to think, joined with reflective study, should be our normal practice as Christians.

A portrait of Michael Faraday hung in Albert Einstein's office. It was Faraday's work that made Einstein a household name. Fields of force, Faraday's brainchild, continues to impact the intellectual world of physics today. Faraday was raised in a Christian home adhering to God's creation of all things. In an 1845 scientific address, Faraday stated his belief that the "various forms under which the forces of matter are made manifest have one common origin."[558] Though not trained as a scientist, he was a collector of what he saw in God's world. Whether one searches for maps or quarks, the very idea of study depends on something to study. Christ Himself is the vault of all earthly wisdom apart from whom no study would be accomplished.

Endnotes

[1] Harold Brodkey, "Reading, the Most Dangerous Game," in *Reading in Bed: Personal Essays in the Glories of Reading*, ed. Steven Gilbar (Boston: David R. Godine, 2007), 104–05.

[2] Sven Birkerts, "The Death of Literature," in *The Gutenberg Elegies: The Fate of Reading in an Electronic Age* (London: Faber and Faber, 1994), 197.

[3] Vigen Guroian, *Rallying the Really Human Things: The Moral Imagination in Politics, Literature, and Everyday Life* (Wilmington, DE: Intercollegiate Studies Institute, 2005), 177–86.

[4] Acts 4:12. Jesus Himself made extraordinary claims about being the only way to eternal salvation. A few of many passages include John 3:18, 5:24, 6:35–40, and 14:6.

[5] Created out of nothing (Romans 4:17), the creation is the personal, intimate (Amos 4:13) work of its Creator (Proverbs 3:19–20, 8:27; Jeremiah 33:2). The sustaining governance of the world's systems has been embedded within creation itself (Psalm 33:9: "stood firm" suggests a governor of creation maintains, supports, and oversees the works of God's hands) evidenced through natural law—the reliable works of God's creation (Job 28:25–26; Psalm 148:6; Proverbs 8:29) that can be known by humans (Job 28:3, 11). In this way, the discovery of knowledge by people is inexhaustible (Job 26, esp. v. 14).

[6] Since we are new creations in Christ (2 Corinthians 5:17), we are created to do good works (Ephesians 2:10) but must appropriate virtuous characteristics to be effective and productive believers (2 Peter 1:3–11). Our responsibilities demand effort to possess virtuous qualities that demonstrate our Christian beliefs.

[7] To encourage young people to "remember the Creator in the days of their youth" (Ecclesiastes 11:9–12:1) is an important foundation stone for life.

[8] Galatians 5:13–6:5.

[9] B. B. Warfield, "The Religious Life of Theological Students" in *Selected Shorter Writings of B. B. Warfield*, vol. 1 (Phillipsburg, NJ: Presbyterian and Reformed, 1911), 414.

[10] A. G. Sertillanges, *The Intellectual Life: Its Spirit, Conditions, Methods.* Trans. Mary Ryan. Fwd., James V. Schall (Washington, D.C.: Catholic University of America Press, 1998), 19.

[11] Jonathan Edwards, "The Importance and Advantage of a Thorough Knowledge of Divine Truth" in *The Great Awakening and American Education* (New York: Teachers College Press, 1973), 207.

[12] Warfield, *Selected Shorter Writings of B. B. Warfield*, 424, 422.

[13] Psalm 119: 47–48, 97, 113, 119, 127, 159, 163, 165, 167.

[14] George J. Zemek, *The Word of God in the Child of God* (Mango, FL: Self Published, n.d.), 233.

[15] Zemek, *The Word of God in the Child of God*, 95.

[16] The first occurrences are in Psalm 119:14, 16.

[17] Derek Kidner, *Psalms 73–150* (Downers Grove: IVP, 1975), 420.

[18] Gary G. Cohen, *Theological Wordbook of the Old Testament* (Chicago: Moody, 1980), 2:873.

[19] Edwards, *The Great Awakening*, 202.

[20] Haddon Robinson, "The Theologian and the Evangelist," *Journal of the Evangelical Society* (March 1985), 3–8.

[21] Howard Hendricks, *Teaching to Change Lives* (Colorado Springs: Multnomah, 2003).

[22] Reference to Samuel Solivan, "Orthopathos: Interlocutor between Orthodoxy and Praxis," *Andover Newton Review* 1 (Winter 1990), 19–25, quoted by Robert W. Pazmino, *By What Authority do we Teach?* (Grand Rapids: Eerdmans, 1994), 120.

[23] A play off the theme addressed by James W. Sire in *Habits of the Mind: Intellectual Life as a Christian Calling.* (Downers Grove: IVP, 2000), 76–77. Sire uses a great many of the ideas found in Sertillanges (above).

[24] Benjamin W. Patton, "Recovered Ground," *Smithsonian* (June 2009), 80–86; excerpt from p. 86.

[25] "E Pluribus Unum," The Bradley Project on America's National Identity, May 25, 2009, www.bradleyproject.org.

[26] "E Pluribus Unum," The Bradley Project on America's National Identity, May 25, 2009, http://www.bradleyproject.org/EPUReportFinal.pdf, pages 4–5.

27 "Episcopalians Are Reaching Point of Revolt," *The New York Times*, December 17, 2006, http://www.nytimes.com/2006/12/17/us/17episcopal.html

28 "Episcopal Churches' Breakaway Evolved Over 30 Years," *The Washington Post*, January 4, 2007, http://www.washingtonpost.com/wp-dyn/content/article/2007/01/03/AR2007010301952_2.html

29 Victor P. Hamilton, *The Theological Wordbook of the Old Testament* (Chicago: Moody, 1980), 2:922.

30 Hosea 13:6; Psalm 106:13.

31 Isaiah 51:13.

32 Ezekiel 20:12, 20; 1 Corinthians 15:54–16:2; Esther 9:27–28; Joshua 4:7; Numbers 15:39–40, 16:26–40; Deuteronomy 11:18.

33 2 Peter 3:5; 2 Peter 1:12–15 (three times); 2 Peter 3:8; 2 Peter 3:2.

34 Vigen Guroian, "On Fairy Tales and the Moral Imagination" in *Rallying the Really Human Things* (Wilmington, DE: Intercollegiate Studies Institute, 2005), 49–62. See also the introduction to his book *Tending the Heart of Virtue: How Classic Stories Awaken a Child's Moral Imagination*.

35 Jonathan V. Last, "The Fog of War: Forgetting What We Once Knew," *The Weekly Standard* (May 2009).

36 Martin Luther, "Whether a Soldier Too Can Be Saved" (1526).

37 Calling is a supernatural, sovereign direction in a believer's life based on the gifting of the Holy Spirit, local church guidance, and providential circumstances.

38 Genesis 10:31–32; Isaiah 46:9–11; Acts 17:26.

39 C. S. Lewis, "Learning in War Time," *The Weight of Glory* (San Francisco: HarperOne, 2009), 58.

40 2 Timothy 4:11; see Acts 15:36–41.

41 See Philippians 3:1–6; Galatians 1:13–2:1.

42 Exodus 2–3.

43 Robert H. Scales, "Studying the Art of War," *The Washington Times Online* (February 2005).

[44] Proverbs 19:2.

[45] Proverbs 17:24.

[46] Genesis 2:5, 15.

[47] Romans 1:21.

[48] 1 Corinthians 8:1–2.

[49] 2 Timothy 3:7.

[50] 1 Corinthians 2:16.

[51] Ecclesiastes 5:18–20; 11:9; 12:13–14.

[52] Proverbs 9:9.

[53] Proverbs 4:1.

[54] Proverbs 4:7.

[55] Genesis 1:28.

[56] Hebrews 13:5.

[57] Titus 1:9.

[58] C. S. Lewis, "Learning in War Time," *The Weight of Glory*, 58.

[59] Eugene Peterson, *Christ Plays in Ten Thousand Places* (Grand Rapids: Eerdmans, 2005), 116.

[60] Deuteronomy 30:11–16.

[61] Interestingly, Exodus 31:3 and 39:43 use the term as well in the discussion of building the tabernacle. The term is repeated in the Ten Commandments, Exodus 20:9–10 (see Leviticus 16:29).

[62] Andrew Bowling, *The Theological Wordbook of the Old Testament* (Chicago: Moody, 1980), 1:465.

[63] The Gnostics, who believed they had special revelation from God, tried to coerce people into following human-centered law. But Paul exploded the falsehood in Colossians 2:16–23, citing the Sabbath as a person-friendly regulation benefiting the individual.

[64] Romans 14 and 1 Corinthians 8 are two passages that establish clear principle and practice of what theologians call "individual soul liberty." What is not commanded in Scripture is left to the personal direction of the Spirit in the life of the Christian.

[65] Some might wonder how eating leftovers is included alongside household chores. Economics (literally, stewardship) necessitates a wise use of all things. If I cannot adequately manage the contents of my own refrigerator, how can I advocate propriety when it comes to anything else? I have a strange sense of satisfaction when a leftover container is placed in the dishwasher from another day's meal.

[66] Genesis 2:3 uses the word "rest," meaning the state or condition for cessation, completion, and ultimately, celebration. Victor P. Hamilton, *Theological Wordbook of the Old Testament* (Chicago: Moody, 1980), 902–03.

[67] The word means to bring a process to completion, to carry out a task in full, to perfection. Paul R. Gilchrist, *Theological Wordbook of the Old Testament* (Chicago: Moody, 1980), 377–78. I still ponder the connection between "it is finished" in Genesis and Jesus' declaration on the cross.

[68] I am indebted to Eugene Peterson's phrase "creation cadence" from *Christ Plays in Ten Thousand Places* (Grand Rapids: Eerdmans, 2005), 114.

[69] The word indicates skilled workmanship relating to one's business, habits, or skills as seen in Exodus 20:9–10, 31:3, 39:43; Leviticus 16:29. Andrew Bowling, *Theological Wordbook of the Old Testament* (Chicago: Moody, 1980), 465.

[70] Born of my delight in the book of Leviticus, I still have the notes from my earliest message: Leviticus 23:3, 22, February 1987, "Beware of Becoming Hollow People." As a reminder, Sabbath does *not* equal Sunday. Sunday was the first day of the week (1 Corinthians 16:1), the day of resurrection, the reason for Christian worship. In the Hebrew mind-set, Sabbath is the seventh day, the last day of the week.

[71] "Worry. Don't Be Happy," *Newsweek*, April, 26, 2008, http://www.newsweek.com/id/45228/

[72] Ecclesiastes 2:24; 3:14; 5:18–20, etc.

[73] Exodus 20:8–11.

[74] Far from being simply "beasts of burden," God's covenant included animals in Genesis 9. During the tenth plague in Egypt, even the firstborn cattle died (Exodus 11:5). When Jonah preached, the animals too were draped in sackcloth (Jonah 3:8). PETA (People for the Ethical Treatment of Animals) cannot hold a candle to the groundbreaking concern for animals in the First Testament.

[75] Leviticus 23:3 says Sabbath was "a day of sacred assembly," our word for convention today.

[76] "Remember" has the idea of establishing a memorial in Exodus 20:8 (NIV). "Keeping" meant to protect, pay attention to, and exercise care for, as in Deuteronomy 5:12.

[77] When the people left Egypt (Leviticus 23:42–43), God was the landlord (25:23) for generations to come (23:41), benefiting descendants (23:33, 42) and demonstrating the possibility of release from debt (25:10).

[78] Exodus 31:12–17; Deuteronomy 15:1–11; Nehemiah 13:15–22; Mark 2:20–28; John 7:21–24; and Colossians 2:16–23.

[79] Leviticus 23:3: "wherever you live."

[80] "A Sabbath to the LORD." Elsewhere, God calls this "MY Sabbath" (Leviticus 26:2; Isaiah 56:4).

[81] Some good cultural background material on the Pharisees and the Sabbath can be had by reading William Barclay's *The Gospel of Matthew, vol. 2* (Louisville: Westminster, 1958), 20–30 and Craig S. Keener's *The IVP Bible Background Commentary on the New Testament* (Downers Grove, IVP, 1995), 77–78, 141–43.

[82] Blaise Pascal, *Pensees,* 130–131.

[83] Arnold Toynbee, "Work, the Great Anesthetic," *Milwaukee Journal* (August 1971).

[84] John H. Walton, et al, *The IVP Bible Background Commentary: Old Testament* (Downers Grove: IVP, 2000), 30.

[85] Victor P. Hamilton, *Theological Wordbook of the Old Testament* (Chicago: Moody, 1980), 2:902.

[86] Worship is to time what a temple is to space.

[87] The word *holy* is in the same grammatical construction as *blessed*. God pronounced a state of holiness within time that, once begun, would continue. Notice in creation that God called other things *good* while time was sanctified.

[88] The blessing of rest is a command that can only be given from the Creator to creation. Time itself was infused with eternal significance: the quality of heaven now asserts itself, woven within the earth.

[89] Hebrews 4:1–10.

[90] This is the best, most readable, solidly biblical volume on both subjects. Leland Ryken, *Work & Leisure in Christian Perspective* (Colorado Springs: Multnomah, 1987), 87–115. Leisure, like anything else, can be twisted for wrong. Latin and French origins indicate the word meant "permission," later becoming *illicit, licentious,* giving way to *license* and *laziness.*

[91] Deuteronomy 5:12–15.

[92] Abraham J. Heschel, *The Sabbath: Its Meaning for Modern Man.* (New York: Farrar, Straus, & Young, 1951), 21, 31–32.

[93] Galatians 4:4; 1 Peter 1:20; Revelation 22:13.

[94] 2 Peter 1:16, 3:4.

[95] 2 Peter 3:8–9, 14–15.

[96] Mireille Guiliano, *French Women Don't Get Fat: The Secret of Eating for Pleasure* (New York: Knopf, 2005), 44.

[97] The noun "diet" has become a verb, giving undo responsibility for doing over being.

[98] "Evaluating Weight Loss Programs: What Are the Red Flags?" *Body Positive,* February 8, 2008, http://www.bodypositive.com/wtloss.htm

[99] "Amid Financial Crunch Health Clubs Get in Shape to Keep Members," *Los Angeles Times,* January 3, 2009, http://articles.latimes.com/2009/jan/03/business/fi-gyms3

[100] Eckhart Tolle, *The Power of Now.* (New York: New World Library, 1999).

[101] Francis A. Schaeffer, *The God Who is There* (Downers Grove: IVP, 1971), 129.

[102] G. K. Chesterton, *Orthodoxy* (London: John Lane Company, 1908), 20.

[103] Henry Zylstra, "Thoughts for Teachers" in *Testament of Vision* (Grand Rapids: Eerdmans, 1958), 173.

[104] "Doctrine" normally refers to specific beliefs (e.g., Christian instruction on sin, salvation, or angels). The New Testament most often uses the word *didaskalia,* meaning "teaching" or "what is learned." The content of teaching can be positive (Romans 15:4) or negative (Colossians 2:22).

[105] "Theology" generally means the comprehensive overview of the church's teaching. Theology encapsulates the whole of a belief system. In the case of the Judeo-Christian viewpoint, everything is theological; all things must be viewed from heaven's perspective.

[106] First Timothy 1:10; cf. Matthew 6:22–23. Medical terms were used as metaphors for the condition of one's spirit or teaching by Greek and Roman writers (Keener, *IVP Bible Background Commentary New Testament*, 609). A salve or medication applied externally is the idea of 1 Timothy 1:8–10. The word "sound" or "healthy" is from the Greek, from whence comes our word "hygienic."

[107] Notice in 1 Timothy 1:8–17 that law has a good function in society, keeping wrongdoing at bay. But sound or healthy doctrine (1:10) comes from God and is entrusted to the church. Notice how many times Paul made a point of saying "this is not about me" in verses 12–17. In fact, he ended with a hymn in verse 17, punctuating the truth.

[108] Deuteronomy 8:10–20; Job 26, 28; Psalm 8:5, 115:1; Ecclesiastes 5:18–20; Romans 11:33–36; Ephesians 5:20; 1 Thessalonians 5:18; 1 Timothy 6:17.

[109] *Seinfeld*, Season 3, Episode 23, first aired May 6, 1992.

[110] It is how Jason Alexander (George) delivers the lines that has me chuckling again even as I type. It is one of many not-to-be-missed *Seinfeld* scenes.

[111] Harry R. Lewis, *Excellence Without a Soul: How a Great University Forgot Education* (Bethesda: Perseus Books Group, 2006).

[112] Isaiah 26:8–9; Psalm 119:20.

[113] Psalm 107:9; Proverbs 19:15, 25:25, 27:7.

[114] Isaiah 56:11, 58:10; Jeremiah 50:19.

[115] Ecclesiastes 2:24; 4:8; 6:2–3, 7, 9; 7:28.

[116] Psalm 42:1. Longing for God's courts (Psalm 84:3), the law (Psalm 119:20), salvation (Psalm 119:81), and the Lord Himself (Psalm 130:5; Lamentations 3:25).

[117] Quoted in Douglas Sloan, *The Great Awakening and American Education* (New York: Teacher's College, 1973), 197–211.

[118] Proverbs 19:2.

[119] Sebastian Moore as quoted by James Houston, *The Heart's Desire: A Guide to Personal Fulfillment* (Oxford: Lion, 1992), 27.

[120] Eugene H. Peterson, *Subversive Spirituality* (Grand Rapids: Eerdmans, 1997), 80–83.

[121] *Ibid.*, 204, 211.

[122] Evelyn Underhill, *Practical Mysticism* (Dover: Dover Publishing, 2000), 15.

[123] "Embedded journalists" is the designation given to newspeople who live with military units during wartime, giving writers access to firsthand reports. Jeff Emauel, "I Love Those Guys," *Wall Street Journal* (May 23, 2007).

[124] Charles Haddon Spurgeon, *Metropolitan Tabernacle Pulpit* (London: Passmore & Alabaster, 1863), 668.

[125] Ancient Christian Commentary on Scripture, InterVarsity Press, September 3, 2009, http://www.ivpress.com/accs/

[126] "In Tough Times Humanities Must Justify Their Worth," *The New York Times*, February 25, 2009, http://www.nytimes.com/2009/02/25/books/25human.html

[127] Vigen Guroian, *Rallying the Really Human Things: Moral Imagination in Literature, Politics, and Everyday Life* (Wilmington, DE: Intercollegiate Studies Institute, 2005), 184–85.

[128] "Bush is a Book Lover," *The Wall Street Journal*, December 26, 2008, http://online.wsj.com/article/SB123025595706634689.html

[129] Kenneth R. Badley, "The Community of Faith as the Locus of Faith-Learning Integration" in *Alive to God: Studies in Spirituality Presented to James Houston*, ed. J.I. Packer and Loren Wilkenson (Downers Grove, IVP, 1992), 292–93.

[130] D. G. Hart, *A Student's Guide to Religious Studies* (Wilmington, DE: Intercollegiate Studies Institute, 2005): 44, 48.

[131] Aquinas (1225–1274) was a Dominican monk. He was a popular teacher who wrote *Summa Theologica*, a summation of theological knowledge. Robert J. Choun, *Evangelical Dictionary of Christian Education* (Grand Rapids: Baker, 2001), 46–47. His industry, depth of thought, and discernment gained him the title "Doctor Angelicus." R. C. Sproul, *The Consequences of Ideas: Understanding the Concepts that Shaped our World* (Wheaton: Crossway, 2000), 65.

[132] Thomas Aquinas, *Summa Theologica* (Chicago: Encyclopedia Brittanica, Inc., 1954), 636.

[133] See, "Discipline: What Kramer Said to George."

[134] With deep admiration and thanks to Gayle, Teresa, Fran, Rod, Travis, Casey, Ken, Blake, Dondi, Doug, and Tommy.

[135] Christine Rosen, "When Books Were Great." *The Weekly Standard* (December 22, 2008), 34.

[136] Ephesians 1:17–18; Philippians 1:9–11; Colossians 1:9–10; 2 Peter 3:18; see 1 Peter 2:2.

[137] Romans 8:29; see John 5:39; 2 Corinthians 3:18; 1 Peter 1:23.

[138] Deuteronomy 4:35–36; 11:2–7; 2 Timothy 3:16.

[139] Proverbs 1:8 (NIV), 8:10; Ephesians 4:11–16.

[140] Galatians 3:24–25; 2 Peter 1:5–6.

[141] Proverbs 3:11–12; see Deuteronomy 8:1–5.

[142] Proverbs 3:11, 23:13.

[143] Proverbs 24:32.

[144] Proverbs 1:22, 8:5, 9:4.

[145] Proverbs 9:6, 14:18, 22:3.

[146] Proverbs 19:25, 21:11, 27:12.

[147] Daniel J. Boorstin, *The Discoverers: A History of Man's Search to Know His World and Himself* (New York: Random House, 1983), xv–xvi. To me, all other histories pale next to Boorstin's three volumes: *The Discoverers, The Creators, The Seekers*. The former librarian of Congress focused on people rather than time periods of history. Find biblical warrant for the passion of knowledge: Job 26, 28; Proverbs 25:2.

[148] Jerry Kramer, *Lombardi: Winning Is the Only Thing* (Chicago: Pocket, 1970), 86.

[149] Caspar W. Weinberger and Wynton C. Hall, *Home of the Brave: Honoring the Unsung Heroes in the War on Terror* (New York: Forge, 2006), 217–18.

[150] *Ibid.*, 201.

[151] For both definition and practice, see Mark Bender, *Operation Excellence: Succeeding in Business and Life—The U. S. Military Way* (New York: ANACOM, 2004) and *www.military-net.com*.

[152] Frank and Ernest by Thaves, March 19, 2009, http://frankandernest.com/cgi/view/display.pl?96-10-06

[153] The normal Hebrew word order of verb-subject-object is obviously inverted in these phrases from the original language: *"The woman* you gave me" and *"The serpent* deceived me."

[154] One has only to turn the pages of Scripture from beginning ("You may ... you may not," Genesis 2:16–17) to end ("I warn everyone who hears the words of this prophecy," Revelation 22:18) to see God's requirements of responsibility, discipline, and duty. Luke 14:25–35 produces the mantra to be repeated moment by moment: "Count the cost ... count the cost."

[155] Titus 1:9; James 3:1.

[156] Proverbs 23:12; 1 Peter 2:17.

[157] Gregory Roper, "Teachers' Guilt," *First Things* 127 (November, 2002), 21–22.

[158] "For Once, Blame the Student," *USA Today*, February 22, 2008, http://usatoday30.usatoday.com/news/opinion/editorials/2006-03-07-forum-students_x.htm

[159] Genesis 3:17–19.

[160] Galatians 5:16–26.

[161] Against laziness: Proverbs 6:6–11, 24:30–34.

[162] Read Psalm 24.

[163] My retelling of the old tale is from James Baldwin's retelling found in William Bennett's *The Book of Virtues* (New York: Simon and Schuster, 1993), 118–19.

[164] "Gratitude," *Christianity Today*, November 22, 2009, http://www.christianitytoday.com/bc/2009/novdec/gratitude.html?start=1

[165] "Thanksgiving Poem—for Franz Wright," *Christianity Today*, November 22, 2009, http://www.christianitytoday.com/bc/2009/novdec/thanksgivingpoem.html

[166] "Still Here After a Rough Year," *Wall Street Journal*, November 20, 2009, http://online.wsj.com/article/SB10001424052748704204304574546093616349588.html?mod=djemEditorialPage

[167] "Gratitude," The Trinity Forum, December 1, 2009, http://www.ttf.org/index/journal/detail/the-importance-of-gratitude/

[168] W.H. Auden, *W. H. Auden: Selected Poems*, "IX For Friends Only (For John and Teckla Clark)" in Auden's multipart poem "Thanksgiving for a Habitat" (New York: Random House, 2007), 280.

[169] Psalm 16:6 (ESV).

[170] Ecclesiastes 2:24–26, 3:13–14, 5:18–20, 8:15, 9:9.

[171] "Mind-set" is defined as a pattern of thinking established through habitual practice of a philosophy.

[172] "Worship" is the total response of the total person to our Lord Jesus. "In all things He shall receive the preeminence" (Colossians 1:18), who has "reconciled all things to Himself" (1:20) that we should do "all things in the name of the Lord Jesus, giving thanks to God the Father through him" (3:17).

[173] Mark 12:30–31.

[174] I.e., 2 Kings 23:24–25.

[175] Gratitude signals acknowledgment that one is responsible to someone else. Christians practice thanks through prayer (Psalm 75:1) in all things (Ephesians 5:20) (cf. Acts 2:42–47, 4:32–36; 2 Thessalonians 2:15–17).

[176] Many thanks to my nephew, Luke, who hunted down the YouTube video for his uncle! Excerpts in this paragraph can be found at *http://www.youtube.com/watch?v=rOtEQB-9tvk*.

[177] The quotes noted here are attributed to these historical figures, accessed in various references. In this case, the statements are taken from Robert A. Emmons' book *Thanks: How Practicing Gratitude Can Make You Happier* (Boston: Houghton-Mifflin, 2008), 15.

[178] Psalm 89:5, cf. Psalms 105, 106, 145.

[179] 2 Samuel 22:50; Psalm 35:18, 28:7, 109:30.

[180] Psalm 86:12, 119:7, 30:12.

[181] Ralph H. Alexander, *Theological Wordbook of the Old Testament* (Chicago: Moody, 1980), 1:364–66.

[182] R. C. Sproul, *Romans: The Righteous Shall Live By Faith* (Wheaton: Crossway, 2009), 203.

[183] "The Tell-tale Heart" and "The Cask of Amontillado" are two of Poe's short stories mentioned here.

[184] John Ayto, *Dictionary of Word Origins* (New York: Arcade, 1990), 359.

[185] Atul Gawande, *Complications: A Surgeon's Notes on an Imperfect Science* (New York: Picador, 2002).

[186] *Ibid.*, 114.

[187] "A Q&A With P.D. James," Amazon.com, December 15, 2009, http://www.amazon.com/Talking-About-Detective-Fiction-James/dp/B0064XBGZU

[188] G. K. Chesterton, "The Secret of Father Brown," *The Collected Works of G. K. Chesterton* (San Francisco: Ignatius, 1986), 217.

[189] Jeremiah 17:9 MSG.

[190] Flannery O'Connor, *Mystery and Manners* (New York: Farrar, Strauss, and Giroux, 1997), 40–42, emphasis mine.

[191] See Glenn W. Barker, *International Standard Bible Encyclopedia*, Vol. 3 (Grand Rapids: Eerdmans, 1986), 451–55; W. L. Liefeld, *Zondervan Pictorial Encyclopedic Dictionary of the Bible*, *Vol. 4* (Grand Rapids: Zondervan, 1976), 332.

[192] 1 Timothy 3:16 MSG, emphasis mine.

[193] Read Matthew 1–2 and Luke 1–2.

[194] William Barclay, *The Gospel of Matthew, Vol 1.* (Louisville: Westminster, 1958), 28.

[195] There is no indication that the statement was actually made; but all indications of Herod's dispatching those who threatened his throne makes the comment bristle with truth. See Craig S. Keener's historical connections in *A Commentary on the Gospel of Matthew* (Grand Rapids: Eerdmans, 1999), 110–12.

[196] John 12:31, 14:30, 16:11; 1 John 5:19.

[197] Genesis 4 marks both the first anticipation of the Child ("I have brought forth a man!" said Eve) and the first attempt to snuff out the messianic lineage when Abel was killed. Seth was literally the substitute, bearing the beacon of hope through the new Adam, Enoch. See Kenneth A. Mathews, *Genesis 1–11:26* (Grand Rapids: Eerdmans, 1996): 290–91. As for "the ancient serpent" read Revelation 12.

[198] Shifra and Pu'a are given more credence and authority in biblical history than the dictator of a superpower. By refusing to name Egypt's king, the writer strips him of his authority. The power shifts from the throne room to the nursery. As to whether or not the two women were Egyptian or Hebrew, see Everett Fox, *The Five Books of Moses* (New York: Shocken, 1995), 259.

[199] Read the book of Ruth.

[200] "Then the dragon was enraged at the woman and went off to make war against the rest of her offspring—those who obey God's commandments and hold to the testimony of Jesus" (Revelation 12:17).

[201] God will use the evil of people to praise Himself (Psalm 76:10). Read Genesis 45:4–11, 50:20.

[202] Frederick Dale Bruner, *Matthew: A Commentary, Vol. 1.* (Grand Rapids: Eerdmans, 2004), 68.

[203] John Lewis Gaddis, *The Cold War: A New History* (New York: Penquin, 2006), 46.

[204] G. K. Chesterton, "The Secret of Father Brown," *The Collected Works of G. K. Chesterton* (San Francisco: Ignatius, 2002), 219.

[205] Alexander Solzhenitsyn, *The Gulag Archipelago: 1918–1956* (New York: Harper Classics, 2002), 312.

[206] Many other voices would concur with the general concern that humans are corruptible: "The Tell-Tale Heart" by Edgar Allen Poe, "The Lifted Veil" by George Eliot, "Rappaccini's Daughter" by Nathaniel Hawthorne, and "The Man That Corrupted Hanleyburg" by Mark Twain.

[207] James Martin, "Merry Marketing," *Wall Street Journal,* December 17, 2009.

[208] Read Isaiah 7–8.

[209] Isaiah "proud," 9:9; "calloused," 6:10; "lose heart," 7:4; "shaken," 7:2 (NIV).

[210] Anton Chekhov, *The Portable Chekhov* (New York: Viking, 1966), 381.

[211] Louis L'Amour, *Education of a Wandering Man* (New York: Bantam, 1989), 100.

[212] John Gardner, *On Moral Fiction,* (New York: Basic, 1978), 106.

[213] A quote from George Bernard Shaw's play *Back to Methuselah.*

[214] T. S. Eliot, Religion and Literature in *Selected Prose of T. S. Eliot* (London: Faber and Faber, 1935), 100.

[215] Flannery O'Connor, *Mystery & Manners* (New York: Farrar, Straus, Giroux, 1969), 162.

[216] Mortimer J. Adler and Charles Van Doren, *How To Read a Book* (New York: Simon and Schuster, 1972), 346.

[217] William W. Klein, Craig L. Blomberg, and Robert L. Hubbard, Jr., *Introduction to Biblical Interpretation* (Nashville: Thomas Nelson, 2004), 24.

218 Hermann J. Austel, *Theological Wordbook of the Old Testament* (Chicago: Moody, 1980), 2:938–39.

219 Robert Coles, *The Call of Stories: Teaching and the Moral Imagination* (Boston: Houghton Mifflin, 1989), 197.

220 Ernest Gordon, *To End All Wars* (Grand Rapids: Zondervan, 2002), 103–106.

221 *Ibid.*, 117–118. The book explains the interpersonal changes that occurred within the culture of the camp, difficult to express by the film of the same title.

222 George Steiner, *George Steiner: A Reader* (Oxford: Oxford University Press, 1984), 36.

223 Jeremiah 23:29.

224 One of my great concerns for the church is that its people have succumbed to the fallacy that business principles are easily transferred to Christian ministry contexts. While there are pieces of truth everywhere in creation, imposition of naturalistic business principles to govern Christian thinking is a leadership lie.

225 Jeremiah 23:36. "My word" is compared to false teaching (23:16–18, 22, 28–30, 36, 38).

226 Isaiah 9:8.

227 Matthew 8:5–13; Luke 7:1–10.

228 A brief overview of Nazi terror against dissent is recounted be Nicholas A. Basbanes, *A Splendor of Letters: The Permanence of Books in an Impermanent World* (New York: Harper Collins, 2003), 124–26.

229 There are no discounting totalitarian dictatorships' attempts to kill intellectuals in their usurpation of a country. China under Mao ZeDong, Russia under Stalin, and Cambodia under Pol Pot are but a few examples to add with Hitler. Reeducation was an additional tact taken by Vietnamese Communists, for instance, after the fall of the South.

230 Ray Bradbury, *Fahrenheit 451* (New York: Ballantine, 1953).

231 George Orwell, *1984* (London: Everyman's Library, 1992), 260.

232 Basbanes, *A Splendor of Letters*, 133–37.

233 There are, of course, those instances of libraries destroyed by fire without human ill will. Leaders of Alexandria, Egypt declared that ships entering its harbor must surrender any books on board. Copied and returned, these new additions were then placed in the

city library. One of the largest losses of texts in world history—both in numbers and importance—occurred when the library at Alexandria was consumed by flame c. AD 230.

234 Edward Feser, "'Too Christian' for Academia?" *National Review* (February 11, 2009).

235 See 2 Kings 22:11–20.

236 Jeremiah 36:26. I had no thought to continue a discussion about book burning until the Spirit prompted me this morning as I write (March 2, 2009) to discuss in the next article that our adversary not only attacks the written record, but also those who produce it.

237 By using the word "solely," I am not discounting the work of the Spirit on lives or the obvious supernatural intervention in history by the personal, eternal Creator, Yahweh. Written records, however, are the means by which the church establishes the authenticity of Jesus: His incarnation, crucifixion, resurrection, ascension, and promised glorification.

238 I have written a curriculum whose subtitle contains this basic assertion: Mark Eckel, *Timeless Truth: An Apologetic for the Historicity, Authenticity, and Authority of The Bible* (Colorado Springs: Purposeful Design, 2001).

239 I include here only some of the many books should be noted to confirm historical documentation of Scripture. F. F. Bruce's *The New Testament Documents: Are They Reliable?*; Craig Blomberg's *The Historical Reliability of The Gospels*; Luke Timothy Johnson and Paul Barnett's *The Birth of Christianity: The First Twenty Years* and *The Real Jesus*; Philip Jenkins's *Hidden Gospels: How the Search for Jesus Lost Its Way*; and Mark D. Thompson's *A Clear and Present Word: The Clarity of Scripture*.

240 Basbanes, *A Splendor of Letters*, 126–28.

241 "Gunman Kills Dutch Film Director," BBC News, accessed November 2, 2004, http://news.bbc.co.uk/2/hi/europe/3974179.stm

242 The cartoon was a satirical comment on the fact that some Muslims commit terrorist acts in the name of Islam and the prophet.

243 Paul Johnson, *Modern Times: The World from the Twenties to the Eighties* (New York: Harper & Row, 1983), 71.

244 Johnson, *Modern Times*, 275ff; 452–54.

245 Any number of quote websites identifies the origin, though one ascribes a dictum very close to this one by Mark Twain. The famed Martin Gilbert in *Churchill: A Life* (New York: Henry Holt, 1991) confirms the essence of Churchill's concern, "It is difficult to overtake slander ... but the truth is very powerful too" (959).

[246] Walid Phares, *Future Jihad: Terrorist Strategies Against America* (Basingstoke: Palgrave MacMillan, 2005), 176–78.

[247] A fifth column is a group that works within its own country against its own country. "Fourth Estate or Fifth Column," accessed January 25, 2005, www.townhall.com. The Pulitzer Prize-winning journalist Peter R. Kann's article "The Power of the Press" examines the ten current trends of mainstream media. Accessed December 13, 2006, http://www. opinionjournal.com/extra/?id=110009377.

[248] A copy of the speech originally given at Reuters headquarters in London on June 12, 2007 was reprinted on June 21, 2007 and is available at *http://www.opinionjournal.com/ extra/?id=110010235*. Jon Stewart, for instance, attacks the character of individuals during *The Daily Show*.

[249] "The word is perverted and debased, to become a catalyst, a drug." Josef Pieper, *Abuse of Language—Abuse of Power* (San Francisco: Ignatius, 1992), 20–23. All who know the power of words should possess this small booklet. For those attune to visual message, watch Robert Redford's *Sneakers:* "It's about who controls the information."

[250] Genesis 4:10–11. See Isaiah 26:21; Matthew 23:31–35; Revelation 6:10; Hebrews 12:24.

[251] Isaiah 26:21. See also Hebrews 12:24; 1 John 3:12–15.

[252] Revelation 6:9–11, 19:14.

[253] Jeremiah 20:9 is the only place in Scripture where an author used the word "fire" for God's Word. God used it in Jeremiah 5:14 and 23:29. See also Exodus 24:17; Deuteronomy 4:24, 9:3; Isaiah 33:14.

[254] James Houston, *Mind on Fire* (Colorado Springs: David C. Cook, 2006), 15.

[255] John 8:32.

[256] Quoted in Edward E. Ericson, Jr. and Alexis Klimoff, *The Soul and Barbed Wire: An Introduction to Solzhenitsyn* (Wilmington, DE: Intercollegiate Studies Institute, 2008), 189.

[257] Robert Fulghum, *From Beginning to End: The Rituals of Our Lives* (New York: Villard, 1995), 27.

[258] Ecclesiastes 9:4. In the Middle East, dogs were considered filthy animals, rejected by humans. A lion, on the other hand, represented the pinnacle of accomplishment, royalty.

[259] Some mistakenly think that the verse gives us *carte blanche* (a blank check) with which to do anything we desire. Others contend this is a statement forwarding the Protestant work

ethic. Still more think the statement mirrors a pessimistic sadness that there is nothing beyond this life. All miss the point.

[260] Springsteen reminded his listeners decades ago not to live in the past or on one's laurels but to consider life's brevity: "gone in the blink of a young girl's eye, glory days."

[261] Jacques Ellul, *Reason for Being: A Meditation on Ecclesiastes* (Grand Rapids: Eerdmans, 1990), 282–83.

[262] Revelation 21:6–7, 9, 18–19.

[263] Revelation 21:16, 20.

[264] Revelation 21:13.

[265] No money to travel? Go places in books! Want to know how others think? Pick up a book! Do you still ask "Why?" Pick up a book! Tired of TV? Pick up a book!

[266] There is much to be said about reading, consuming, and internalizing God's Word. "Eating the Word" (Jeremiah 15:16 and Ezekiel 2:9–3:3) has been a mantra in my teaching since 1983. "Sweet words" is a concept repeated about Scripture consistently (Psalm 119:103 and Proverbs 24:13–14). Most recently, Eugene Peterson reflected on the teaching in his *Eat This Book: A Conversation in the Art of Spiritual Reading* (Grand Rapids: Eerdmans, 2006).

[267] Lee Iacocca and William Novak, *Iacocca: An Autobiography* (New York: Bantam, 1986), 18.

[268] Separated by a vowel, the difference between "business" and "busyness" is no fluke. The original meaning of the old English word "busy" communicated anxiety and unease. "The chief business of the American people is business," famously stated by Calvin Coolidge in 1925, has usurped our psyche. Now it seems the chief business of the American people is busyness. John Ayto, *Arcade Dictionary of Word Origins.* (New York: Little and Brown, 1990), 88; *Word Mysteries & Histories* (Boston: Houghton-Mifflin), 28.

[269] Quoted in *The Wounded Leader* by Ackerman and Maslin-Ostrowski (Hoboken: Jossey-Bass, 2002), 6.

[270] Eugene Peterson, *The Contemplative Pastor* (Grand Rapids: Eerdmans, 1993), 17–25.

[271] Daniel J. Boorstin, *Cleopatra's Nose: Essays on the Unexpected* (New York: Vintage, 1995), 162–63.

[272] See for example Psalm 5:1; Isaiah 38:14, 59:11; and Lamentations 3:62. *Onomatopoeia* is a word that imitates the sound it seems to convey. In this case, the word for reflection sounds like a sigh.

273 Psalm 2:1; Proverbs 24:2.

274 Proverbs 15:28.

275 Herbert Wolf, *Theological Wordbook of the Old Testament* (Chicago: Moody, 1980), 1:205. "Meditation" is amplified by "words"—thoughts and verbal communication. The Psalmist compared God's speech with his own.

276 Willem A. VanGemeren, *Psalms*. In the *Expositor's Bible Commentary* (Grand Rapids: Zondervan, 1991), 740. 1 Chronicles 16:9; Psalm 105:2.

277 Proverbs 6:20–22. Note the threefold repetitious element of ingrained character impacting all the hours of the day. Gary G. Cohen, *Theological Wordbook of the Old Testament* (Chicago: Moody, 1980), 2:875–76.

278 By this, the authors mean "all the time": Joshua 1:8; Psalms 1:2, 119:97, 99. Some passages suggest that this occurs during sleepless hours: Psalms 4:4, 63:6, 77:6.

279 Psalms 77:12, 119:27, 145:5. Herein is the problem with Eastern religions: meditation on nothing.

280 Job 28:15–16.

281 *Keil* and *Delitzsch* suggest musical alteration, as in moving from *piano* to *forte*. (Grand Rapids: Eerdmans, 1978), V:103. See also Walton, *et al., The IVP Bible Background Commentary: Old Testament* (Downers Grove: IVP, 2001), 517–18.

282 Saint Benedict developed the fourfold order of Scripture reading in the sixth century: *lectio, meditatio, oratio, contemplatio.* Benedict did not desire a separation between them but to have them function together. Luther, Calvin, and the Puritans all practiced some form of thoughtful reflection.

283 Some think that *selah* may have been an indication that other Scriptures should be read for biographical background or commentary. Geoffry W. Grogan, *Psalms* (Grand Rapids: Eerdmans, 2008), 30, 38. While scholars debate the origin and meaning of the term, most would agree that *selah* was introduced in strategic spots for a musical rest or a break in the song.

284 *Hamah* in verse 3 is a strong word with strong feeling, based on unrest and turbulence, ending in a loud noise. Carl Philip Weber, *Theological Wordbook of the Old Testament* (Chicago: Moody, 1980), 1:219.

285 Gary G. Cohen, *Theological Wordbook of the Old Testament* (Chicago: Moody, 1980), 2:875–76.

[286] Verse 3 directly connects the author's pain with God. His spirit is faint, weak. Verse 6 indicates a comparison with better times.

[287] The Hebrew word is *chaphas*, meaning to check out or trace. In Psalm 64:6, the word is used three times—the noun occurs with the pual participle, indicating a diligent, deep search, an investigation of everything. In Psalm 77, the Hebrew Piel stem suggests concrete situations are in order; there is something specific in our search, though it may not be found. Herbert Wolf *Theological Wordbook of the Old Testament* (Chicago: Moody, 1980), 1:312.

[288] Thomas E. McComiskey, *Theological Wordbook of the Old Testament* (Chiago: Moody, 1980), 1:241–43.

[289] Robert J. Radcliffe and Julie Gorman, *Evangelical Dictionary of Christian Education* (Grand Rapids: Baker, 2001), 583–84.

[290] Restitution, chaos, and quest are the three major narrative types suggested. Richard H. Ackerman and Paul Maslin-Ostrowski, *The Wounded Leader* (Hoboken: Jossey-Bass, 2002), 95–105.

[291] Note the decisive shift from a focus on "I" (verses 1–13)—sixteen times, and twenty-two times with "me, my"—to "You" (verses 11–20)—twenty times.

[292] Rainer Maria Rilke, *Letters to a Young Poet* (New York: New World Library, 2000), 26.

[293] I am *not* saying thought is unimportant, work is wrong, accomplishment is irrelevant, human effort is unnecessary, or suffering is negligible. I am saying to read Job 40:4–5 and 42:1–6.

[294] Verse 10 is the *chiasmic center* of the Psalm, meaning the pinnacle or focal point of Hebraic poetic form.

[295] Psalm 77:10–20. J. I. Packer said it best: "Meditation is the activity of calling to mind, and thinking over, and dwelling on, and applying to oneself, the various things that one knows about the works and ways and purposes and promises of God … It is an activity of holy thought, consciously performed in the presence of God, under the eye of God, by the help of God, as a means of communion with God." J. I. Packer, *Knowing God* (Downers Grove: IVP, 1973), 18–19.

[296] Flannery O'Connor, *Mystery and Manners* (New York: Macmillan, 1997), 77–78.

[297] John E. Hartley, *Theological Wordbook of the Old Testament* (Chicago: Moody, 1980), 2:791–92 and Paul R. Gilcrist, *Theological Wordbook of the Old Testament* (Chicago: Moody, 1980), 1:373–74.

[298] Psalm 42:5, 11; 43:5; 130:7.

[299] Jeremiah 14:8, 17:13, 50:7.

[300] Job 13:15.

[301] Glenn Tinder, *The Fabric of Hope: An Essay* (Druid Hills, GA: Emory University Press, 1999), 123. Tinder's philosophical commentary should be read by all interested Christians intending to invest their lives in political life.

[302] John Anderson. "After a Devastating Loss, A New Subtext." *New York Times* (August 10, 2008: AR9).

[303] Recipes ("the eyes of all look to you, and you give them their food in due season," Psalm 145:15); incidents ("when David hid in the cave," Psalm 57); news items ("He saved them from the hand of the foe," Psalm 106:10); reprint prayers (Psalm 132:8–10; 2 Chronicles 6:41), cries of agony (about others' slander, Psalm 7); calls for retribution (Psalm 137); ponderings (Psalm 107); opines on international intrigue (Psalm 18); rejoicings in good things (Psalm 136); poetry recitation (Psalm 45:1); comments on the weather (Psalm 147); remarks about creation ("even the sparrow has found a home," Psalm 84:3); remembrances of historical events (Psalm 78); and considerations from the obituary page (Psalm 90).

[304] Psalm 104:34. A corollary usage appears in a sarcastic tone from Elijah to the prophets of Baal: "perhaps your god is musing" (1 Kings 18:27). The suggestion in context seems to be a leisurely approach to life without much thought to action. The positive idea of the word "musing"—individual reminiscing about life—perhaps best carries the meaning. Gary G. Cohen, *Theological Wordbook of the Old Testament* (Chicago: Moody, 1980), 2:875-76.

[305] *ordo, ordiri.* Joseph T. Shipley, *Dictionary of Word Origins* (New York: Philosophical Library, 1945), 33–34, 251.

[306] Alexander Pope, "An Essay On Man," *The Harvard Classics* (London: Collier, 1910), 40:442.

[307] Richard M. Weaver, *Visions of Order: The Cultural Crisis of Our Time* (Wilmington, DE: Intercollegiate Studies Institute, 1995). Russell Kirk's *The Roots of American Order* (Washington, D.C.: Regnery, 1992) is dependent upon Weaver's work. Surprisingly, Kirk gives his friend Weaver no credit for the seminal ideas he records about "order" on pages 4–6.

[308] Jane Jacobs, *The Death and Life of Great American Cities* (New York: Modern Library, 1993), 485–510.

[309] *The Message* translation.

[310] *The Collected Poems* entitled "My-Ness" (437).

[311] Eric Clapton, *Clapton: The Autobiography* (New York: Broadway, 2007), 3–26.

[312] As quoted by James H. Cone, *The Spiritual & The Blues: An Interpretation* (Evanston, IL: Seabury, 1972), 6.

[313] Steve Turner, *Hungry for Heaven: Rock 'n' Roll & the Search for Redemption* (Downers Grove: IVP, 1995), 40–42.

[314] Cone, *The Spiritual & The Blues*, 20, 32.

[315] Steven D. Brookfield, *Becoming a Critically Reflective Teacher* (Hoboken: Jossey-Bass, 1995). Mezirow, Jack, "Learning to Think Like an Adult: Core Concepts of Transformation Theory," *Learning as Transformation: Critical Perspectives on a Theory in Progress* (Hoboken: Jossey-Bass, 2000), 3–33.

[316] Metaphors are used by Donald Schön and Joseph Dunne quoted in Doug Blomberg, *Wisdom and Curriculum*, (Sioux Center, IA: Dordt Press, 2007), 7–8.

[317] Romans 5:1–5.

[318] Cone, *The Spiritual & The Blues*, 32.

[319] Compare the spiritual with Psalm 31:9–13.

[320] The song comes from Psalm 55, specifically verse 6.

[321] Jan Wenner, "Bono—The Rolling Stone Interview," *Rolling Stone* (November 3, 2005).

[322] Cone, *The Spiritual & The Blues*, 32–33, 46.

[323] Ecclesiastes 1:16; 2:1, 15, etc.

[324] Ecclesiastes 7:23.

[325] Ecclesiastes 7:27, 29; 12:9; 6:11–12. See Mark Eckel, "A Story of Transformation: Ecclesiastes as an Example of Adult Learning Processes," *Intégrité* 7:2 (Fall 2008), 42–52.

[326] While this scenario sounds caustic in print, it was always well received in person. Shocking a student into thinking through what he or she was saying, supported by the class majority, taught an important lesson.

[327] Robert L. Alden, *Proverbs: A Commentary on an Ancient Book of Timeless Advice* (Grand Rapids: Baker, 1983), 57.

[328] Proverbs 21:26. Robert L. Alden, *The Theological Wordbook of the Old Testament* (Chicago: Moody, 1980), 1:18.

[329] Proverbs 13:4; 21:26.

[330] When speaking to teachers, I sometimes have to remind them *not* to teach a lesson and then announce, "Now let's do something fun!" The obvious suggestion is that learning is *not* fun, something simply to get through so that we can have "fun."

[331] Proverbs 12:11. "Fantasy" is translated as "worthless pursuits" by the English Standard Version (ESV).

[332] William White, *The Theological Wordbook of the Old Testament* (Chicago: Moody, 1980), 2:834.

[333] See my earlier articles in the Study series on student as vocation.

[334] Cornelius Plantinga, *Engaging God's World: A Christian Vision of Faith, Learning, and Living* (Grand Rapids: Eerdmans, 2002), 139–40. Everyone should read this book: a popular overview of substantive Christian thought.

[335] Steven Johnson, "How Twitter Will Change the Way We Live," *TIME* (June 5, 2009).

[336] Bonnie Rochman, "Twittering in Church, with the Pastor's O.K.," *TIME* (May 3, 2009).

[337] Blaise Pascal, *Pensees*, 139.

[338] Norman Cousins, quoted by Thomas V. Morris, *Making Sense of It All: Pascal and the Meaning of Life* (Grand Rapids: Eerdmans, 1992), 36.

[339] C. S. Lewis, *Screwtape Letters* (New York: MacMillan, 1959), Letter 27.

[340] The cultural impact of distraction is nowhere better overviewed than in *The Listening Heart: Vocation and the Crisis of Modern Culture* by A. J. Conyers (Dallas: Spence, 2006), 52–67.

[341] Maggie Jackson, *Distracted: The Erosion of Attention and the Coming Dark Age* (New York: Prometheus, 2008).

[342] *Gesenius Hebrew Grammar*, E. Kautzsch, ed. (Oxford: Clarendon, 1910), paragraph 159aa.

[343] Bruce Waltke, *An Old Testament Theology: An Exegetical, Canonical, and Thematic Approach* (Grand Rapids: Zondervan, 2007), 43–45.

[344] Waltke, *An Old Testament Theology*, 44.

[345] Caitlin Flanagan, "Cultivating Failure," *The Atlantic Monthly* (January/February 2010), 101–11.

346 "Secular Education, Catholic Values," *The New York Times*, March 10, 2009, http://www.nytimes.com/2009/03/09/nyregion/09charter.html

347 "Look Ahead with Stoicism—And Optimism," *The Wall Street Journal*, December 31, 2009, wsj.com/article/SB10001424052748704152804574628522483219740.html?mod=djemEditorialPage

348 "Goodbye, Google," Stop Design, March 20, 2009, http://stopdesign.com/archive/2009/03/20/goodbye-google.html

349 Over the last years, I've been using a hyphen to designate that which should be inseparable. An example would include "faith-learning integration." My belief is wedded with study.

350 Numbers 14:24, 32:12; Joshua 1:36.

351 Robert Jay Lifton, *Nazi Doctors: Medical Killing and the Psychology of Genocide* (New York: Basic, 1988), 98.

352 See my article: Mark Eckel, "Selling the School: A Christian Response to the Consumer Education Model," *Christian Educators Journal* (February 2009), 28.

353 Neil Postman, *Technopoly: The Surrender of Culture to Technology* (New York: Knopf, 1992), 185–86.

354 Proverbs 20:15, 30:7–9.

355 Tod Lindberg, "The Deepest Roots," *National Review* (August 10, 2009), 41.

356 John H. Zenger and Joseph Folkman, *The Extraordinary Leader: Turning Good Managers into Great Leaders* (Chicago: McGraw-Hill, 2002): 80, 186, 234, 260.

357 *Ibid.*, 63–65.

358 *Ibid.*, 14, 64–65, 232, 256.

359 Proverbs 15:14, 18:15, 19:25, 22:17–18.

360 Deuteronomy 6:10–12 reminds the people that God gave a land ready for inhabitation. It is good to be reminded of the "you did not" phrases (cf. 8:10–20). James 4:13–17 is clear.

361 For example: Psalm 115:1; Matthew 25:34–40; 2 Corinthians 8:1–5.

362 1 Corinthians 10:4; Hebrews 3:6, 14, 6:11; Revelation 2:26, 21:6, 22:13.

[363] Quoted by Miles Harvey in *The Island of Lost Maps: A True Story of Cartographic Crime* (New York: G.K. Hall, 2001), 24–25.

[364] I taught what I called *CLAWS,* or "Christian Life and World Studies" in Christian high schools for seventeen years. Most Christian schools refer to this as "Bible class."

[365] "Academic rigor" is an educational phrase that should be heard more often in school halls. See Louis Markos, "Wrestling in the Academy: How Christian Professors Can Train Their Students to Grapple with Ideas," *Intégrité: A Faith and Learning Journal* 4:2 (Fall 2005), 16–22

[366] Marvin Wilson, *Theological Wordbook of the Old Testament* (Chicago: Moody, 1980), 2:574.

[367] Proverbs 4:20; 5:1, 13; 22:17.

[368] 1 Kings 11:2–4, 9; 2 Samuel 19:14.

[369] A few examples include Jeremiah 7:24, 26; 11:8; 17:23.

[370] Joshua 24:23.

[371] Colin Duriez, *Francis Schaeffer: An Authentic Life* (Wheaton: Crossway, 2008), 103–26.

[372] Blaise Pascal, *Pensees,* number 821.

[373] See, for instance, *Lost and Philosophy: The Island Has Its Reasons* (Hoboken: Wiley-Blackwell, 2007). Twenty-one philosophers discuss the deep, human questions raised by the *Lost* series.

[374] Luke 10:25–37.

[375] For example, the "wise men" noted via the incarnation story most probably traveled with a sizeable retinue, including servants, which would have made their group much larger than the three figures normally included in Christmas manger scenes.

[376] Numbers 21:4; Isaiah 40:3.

[377] Psalm 39:1; Proverbs 2:12–15.

[378] Ezekiel 7:3, 8; 18:30; 22:31; 33:20 with 3:18; 13:22; 18:23; 33:8, 11. The New Testament word *hodos* is used much the same way as *derek* in the First Testament to describe a pathway. The unique metaphorical phrasing indicates a direction or manner of life.

[379] The book of Deuteronomy is the fifth most quoted book in the New Testament. The fact that Jesus quoted exclusively from Moses' last book to turn back temptation suggests its strength. Orthodox Jewish homes remind everyone of Deuteronomy's importance, as

the *shema* is affixed to every doorpost. William Sanford LaSor, *et al., Old Testament Survey* (Grand Rapids: Eerdmans, 1982), 188.

[380] Deuteronomy 30:15–16. "Two ways" dominates the book of Proverbs with a device known as *antithetic parallelism*. As one reads Proverbs, one life choice is contrasted to another, most often with the word "but." Different options include: wisdom versus folly, righteousness versus wickedness, and life versus death.

[381] Deuteronomy 5:33, 8:6, 10:12, 11:22, 13:5, 19:9, 26:17, 28:9, 29:19, 30:16. See also Joshua 22:5; 1 Kings 2:3, 3:14, 8:58, 11:38, 16:31; 2 Chronicles 6:27, 31.

[382] Of course, one can always walk contrary to the ways of God, as pointed out in Leviticus 26:3, 12, 21, 23–24, 27–28.

[383] Ronald J. Williams, *Hebrew Syntax: An Outline* (Toronto: University of Toronto Press, 1980), 46

[384] E. Kautzsch, *Gesenius' Hebrew Grammar* (Oxford: Clarendon, 1980), 380.

[385] These ways must be taught (Isaiah 2:3; Micah 4:2) because they bear the name of the Lord (Micah 4:5). A voice will remind the walker, "This is the way; walk in it" (Isaiah 30:21). Authority is given those who adhere to the path (Zechariah 3:7).

[386] See the three stories Jesus told about "lost and found" in Luke 15.

[387] Luke 15:4.

[388] Over fifty times in the Gospels, beginning with Matthew 4:19, people physically followed Jesus.

[389] For those who know or remember, Dana and Mantey's famous "Diagram of the Directive and Local Functions of Prepositions" in their *A Manual Grammar of the Greek New Testament* is the best visual picture to communicate prepositional usage (New York: Macmillan, 1950), 113.

[390] The normal preposition in Hebrew means accompaniment or instrumentation. Now it is possible to say you are *with* someone when it is not true. The Lord calls His people out this way by saying, "Seek good, not evil, that you may live. Then the Lord God Almighty will be with you, *just as you say He is*" (Amos 5:14).

[391] Comments there about the durative action of the Hebrew verb hold true in Genesis 3:8; 5:22, 24; 6:9.

[392] Genesis 5:22, 24; 6:9.

[393] Seth is literally the meaning of his name—Abel's "replacement."

[394] Bruce K. Waltke gives a superb, structural overview of the text in question. *Genesis: A Commentary* (Grand Rapids: Zondervan, 2001), 109–120.

[395] J. G. McConville, *Deuteronomy* in *The Apollos Old Testament Commentary* (Downers Grove: IVP, 2002), 233–244. It is impossible to communicate in a short article the importance of the word, idea, and application of "covenant."

[396] Abraham and Isaac: Genesis 17:1, 24:40, 48:15; Psalm 56:13.

[397] 1 Kings 14:8 and 2 Kings 23:3.

[398] Zechariah 8:23.

[399] Genesis 5:22, 24; 6:9; 17:1; 24:40; 48:15. "Covenantal people" should be committed, no matter what.

[400] Haggai 2:4.

[401] "Walking: Trim Your Waistline, Improve Your Health," The Mayo Clinic, March 1, 2009, http://www.mayoclinic.com/health/walking/HQ01612

[402] "Exercise Promotes Longevity and Mental Health," Red Orbit, March 1, 2009, http://www.redorbit.com/news/health/1334940/exercise_promotes_longevity_and_mental_health/index.html

[403] The Walking Site, March 1, 2009, http://www.thewalkingsite.com/

[404] Riverhead Publishers, 2008.

[405] See Mark 7:5; Acts 21:21; Hebrews 13:9. A deep sadness grips me when I see modern Bible translations lose the impact of the words in the original language. *Walk* gives us a picture; *live* (the common translation) is just the idea. *The English Standard Version* captures both the intention and direction in its word-for-word rendition. The best thought-for-thought translation of the text remains Eugene Peterson's *The Message*. Read, for example, how *walk* is rendered in Ephesians 4:1: "I want you to get out there and walk—better yet, run!—on the road God called you to travel."

[406] Leon Morris, *The First and Second Epistles to the Thessalonians*, NICNT (Grand Rapids: Eerdmans, 1959), 118.

[407] See Genesis 3:24; 6:12.

[408] God told Abram in Genesis 12:1 to *walk* (often, unfortunately, translated "go") to a new land so that Abram might *walk* before God (Genesis 17:1).

[409] One of the earliest Christian books was entitled *Didache* or "teaching." The metaphor of choosing between two "ways" or *walking* down two "roads" is a constant recurrence in the text.

[410] Benno Jacob, quoted by Allen P. Ross in his inestimable commentary on Genesis *Creation and Blessing* (Grand Rapids: Baker, 1988), 331.

[411] W. E. Vine, *The Expository Dictionary of New Testament Words* (Grand Rapids: Bethany, 1984), 1207. Beginning in Galatians 5:16, the full list follows: Ephesians 2:2, 10; 4:1, 17; 5:2, 8, 15; Philippians 3:17–18; Colossians 1:10; 2:6; 3:7; 4:5; 1 Thessalonians 2:12; 4:1, 12; 2 Thessalonians 3:6, 11; 1 John 1:6–7; 2:6, 11; 2 John 4, 6; 3 John 3–4.

[412] G. Kittel, *Theological Dictionary of the New Testament* (Grand Rapids: Eerdmans, 1977), V. 944.

[413] Just from the book of Ephesians, we have this list: 2:2, 10–11, 13; 4:1, 17, 22; 5:2, 8, 15.

[414] Galatians 5:16; Romans 13:13; 2 John 4; Ephesians 5:2; Colossians 4:5; 2 Thessalonians 3:6; 2 John 6; Ephesians 2:10. Notice our habits are not described as an external list of "do's and don'ts" but rather those matters which proceed out of one's inner life. This includes the "good works" of Ephesians 2:10 that are totally of God, by God, and through God in the context.

[415] Philippians 1:27; Colossians 1:10; 1 Thessalonians 2:12; and 3 John 6 are just a few of the many references to *walking* as it pleases God. The Greeks emphasized service in the interests of others for the political commonwealth. Moulton and Milligan, *The Vocabulary of the Greek New Testament* (Grand Rapids: Eerdmans, 1976), 75. That type of service was as common then as it is now. But the New Testament emphasis is on the intentions of one's will, seen through our emotions and decisions.

[416] Run, do not *walk*, to buy this book from InterVarsity Press (2006). I continue to ingest pages 31–50.

[417] Michael Youssef, *Divine Discontent: Pursuing the Peace Your Soul Longs For* (New York: Waterbrook Press, 2004), 5.

[418] John Piper, *The Hidden Smile of God* (Wheaton: Crossway, 2001), 80–119. This chapter is quite disturbing in that Cowper was given to suicidal tendencies. Piper's fine research, however, cautions us not to cast aspersions or jump to conclusions because of a man's mental state about a man's eternal state.

[419] Psalm 13:1–2.

[420] Numbers 6:24–26.

[421] Psalm 119:107. The Hebrew word "much" has the idea of very, great, exceeding, or totally, most well known for its use in Genesis 1:31: "God saw His creation—it was very good. For the mathematician, the idea may be best communicated by the phrase "to the nth degree." The word "suffered" (NIV) is from the Niphal stem, suggesting a reflexive, self-oriented idea. To be self-afflicted could mean, as some commentators suggest, contrition or humility in repentance. But the context indicates no personal sin, rather outside persecution. "Suffered much" means we are brought low, knocked down—in some ways, humiliated by our circumstances.

[422] Psalm 119:104; see also v. 101.

[423] Psalm 119:110.

[424] Meaning he is in jeopardy of losing his life: Psalm 119:109; Judges 12:3; 1 Samuel 19:5, 28:21; Job 13:14.

[425] Psalm 119:25, 87.

[426] Solomon agreed that God's teaching is a lamp giving light, leading down the way of life (Proverbs 6:23).

[427] Hebrews 11:1–16.

[428] Psalm 119 is an alphabetical Psalm, divided into the twenty-two letters of the Hebrew alphabet. If read in Hebrew, each verse in a given letter's section would begin with that letter. Verses 105–113 begin with the Hebrew letter "nun" or "n."

[429] "To the end" can mean consequence or reward at the end of life (Psalm 19:11). Derek Kidner, *Psalms 73–150. Tyndale Old Testament Commentary* (Downers Grove: IVP, 1975), 425. But the context seems clear that the Psalmist intends he will continue on through to the end of his lifetime (Psalm 119:33, 44).

[430] As of this writing, Suu Kyi has announced her intention to run for the presidency of her country after years of suffrage as a political prisoner.

[431] Victor P. Hamilton, *The Book of Genesis: Chapters 1–17* (Grand Rapids: Eerdmans, 1990), 192, n. 3. The *hithpael* in Hebrew tells of a durative, continuous action.

[432] Some have suggested that what was heard was God's voice, not His actual movement. While there is some substance to the idea that hearing someone's approach can be understood as hearing someone speak, 2 Samuel 5:24, 1 Kings 14:6, etc. use the same Hebrew construction for the noise of footfalls. To this point, some have suggested this and other physical manifestations of God were the pre-incarnate, second person of the Trinity, Jesus.

Walton, *et al.* ties the word "sound" to "thunder," contending from Zephaniah 2:2 that God was coming in judgment, a precursor to the couple "hiding," as he suggests in *The IVP Bible Background Commentary: Old Testament* (Downers Grove: IVP, 2000), 32.

[433] Theologians refer to an appearance of God as a theophany. Exodus 33:20–24:3 records an example as God said, "You can see my aftereffects, the results but the very presence of God you cannot see."

[434] Genesis 5:22, 24.

[435] "Walk" is the metaphor for personal relationship with God.

[436] Genesis 4:12, 14, 16 all record the idea that Cain "wandered away" from God. "The land of Nod" was a name that meant to wander: literally, Cain was going to wander in the land of wandering. On the other hand, Enoch "traveled with" God as in Genesis 5:22, 24.

[437] Leonard J. Coppes, *Theological Wordbook of the Old Testament* (Chicago: Moody, 1980), 560–61.

[438] Exodus 25:8.

[439] Deuteronomy 23:12–14. Laws governing toilet habits prompted God to say, "Your God moves about in your camp." Second Samuel 7:6–7 records the other Old Testament statement that God moves amongst His people, also in a building context. The end result was that God's people could walk with heads held high.

[440] The English word "lived" or "dwelt" does not capture the Hebrew concept that is clearly passed into the Greek language here in John 1:14.

[441] Hebrews 2:9, 14–18; 4:14–16.

[442] Hebrews 5:23–28.

[443] Hebrews 9.

[444] Psalm 44:18.

[445] Psalm 119:104.

[446] Psalm 119:105.

[447] Psalm 119:35, 37.

[448] Psalm 119:133.

449 *Valley of Vision,* (Edinburgh: Banner of Truth, 1975), 35.

450 Of course, the verse ends, "But you said, 'We will not walk in it.'" The opposite is also true: "My people have forgotten me; they burn incense to worthless idols, which made them stumble in their ways and in the ancient paths. They made them walk in bypaths and on roads not built up" (Jeremiah 18:15).

451 1 Kings 2:3, 8:58; Psalm 119:1, 3, 14, 27, 30, etc.

452 Deuteronomy 5:33, 8:6, 10:12, 11:22, 19:9, etc.

453 Job 23:11; Psalms 18:21, 44:18 with Psalms 25:4; 27:11, 86:11, 119:33, 143:8.

454 Genesis 18:19; 1 Samuel 12:23; 1 Kings 8:36; 2 Chronicles 6:27, etc. with Genesis 6:12; Numbers 22:32; Judges 2:19; 1 Kings 13:33; 15:26, etc.

455 2 Peter 2:15; Jude 11.

456 2 Peter 2:2, 15, 21.

457 Psalm 139:3; Proverbs 5:21.

458 Hebrews 10:20; John 14:6.

459 Eugene H. Peterson, *The Jesus Way: A Conversation on the Ways that Jesus is The Way* (Grand Rapids: Eerdmans, 2007), 39–40.

460 Washington first declared a national day of thanksgiving and prayer while Lincoln officially made Thanksgiving a national holiday.

461 The tale is well told in John Adair's *Founding Fathers: The Puritans in England and America* (Grand Rapids: Baker, 1982), 105–126. Of course, the primary source *Of Plymouth Plantation* by William Bradford is a moving account of God's providence overseeing the (humanly speaking) good and bad of the original English Cape Cod Colony.

462 *The Oxford Companion to United States History,* ed. Paul S. Boyer (Oxford: Oxford University Press, 2001), 598–99.

463 "Foreigner" in *Tyndale Bible Dictionary* (Carol Stream, IL: Tyndale House, 2008, 493) offers a fine overview of how Scripture addresses the issue of the alien living in one's homeland and how to act when a believer finds himself or herself in another country.

464 Hebrews 11:13 suggests that believers in general only see their true home at a distance. See also 1 Peter 2:11–12.

465 Mark Noll, *The Old Religion in a New World* (Grand Rapids: Eerdmans, 2002), 38–39. *The Mayflower Compact* (1620) should still be studied today for the necessity of social cohesion.

466 Walton, *et al.*, *The Old Testament Background Commentary* (Downers Grove: IVP, 2000), 103, 186–87, 518. Exodus 23:17 and Deuteronomy 16:9–16 discuss the annual Israelite pilgrimages. Not uncommon in the ancient world, pilgrims paid subservience (vassal) to the king (suzerain), reaffirming one's loyalty as an individual or nation.

467 Genesis 3:24.

468 Genesis 38:21, 45:23; Exodus 4:24; Genesis 24:21.

469 Walter Brueggemann, *The Land: Place as Gift, Promise, and Challenge in Biblical Faith*, 2nd edition (Minneapolis: Fortress), 3, 5.

470 "Hinduism Spirituality," God Realized, February 1, 2009, http://www.godrealized.com/

471 The explanation given for a "life as a journey" wall clock is available at "Life is a Journey Wall Clock," Café Press, April 5, 2009, http://www.cafepress.com/+life-is-a-journey+clocks?cat=100164

472 "Anime" most often refers to artwork in comic books and video animation with a Japanese origin. One characteristic of anime is characters with large, doe-like eyes. Anime cartoons had early success in the 1980s and have a plethora of online sites and television shows for both child and adult storylines.

473 "Destination or Journey?" Animanachronism, May 1, 2009, http://animanachronism. wordpress.com/2008/10/08/destination-or-journey/

474 Proverbs 2:13, 4:11.

475 Proverbs 2:8; Isaiah 40:14.

476 Psalm 16:11; Proverbs 2:19, 5:6, 15:24.

477 1 Kings 13:33; 2 Kings 8:27; 2 Peter 2:15; 2 Chronicles 11:17; 1 Corinthians 4:17.

478 Job 14:7–14; 19:24–27. Job is possibly the oldest book in the Old Testament; hence its position here.

479 Psalms 16, 39, 49, 73, etc.

480 2:17–3:5, 4:1–6. The latter section is a prophecy of John the Baptist as "Elijah" and Jesus as "the sun of righteousness."

[481] John 14:1–4.

[482] For instance, Matthew 5–7.

[483] Matthew 7:13–14.

[484] "My sheep hear my voice" (John 10:16).

[485] John 14:6, 10:10.

[486] Isaiah 55:7–9.

[487] Alan Jacobs, *Looking Before and After: Testimony and the Christian Life* (Grand Rapids:Eerdmans, 2008), 80.

[488] Job 28:1–11.

[489] Job 26:1–14.

[490] Job 28:12–28.

[491] Isaiah 43:16.

[492] Job 38:20.

[493] Job 19:8.

[494] Job 30:13.

[495] Psalm 142:3.

[496] Lamentations 3:2, 9.

[497] Psalm 119:101; Job 6:14–23.

[498] Isaiah 55:7–9.

[499] Luke 22:42.

[500] Matthew 6:10.

[501] Psalm 27:11; see 18:33, 143:10.

[502] Isaiah 40:3–4; Malachi 3:1; 4:5; Mark 1:2–3; Luke 1:76; John 1:22–23.

[503] "Harak" in *Theological Wordbook of the Old Testament, Vol. 1,* (Chicago: Moody, 1980), 71.

[504] Isaiah 42:16.

[505] Acts 9:2; 19:8, 23; 22:4; 24:14, 22.

[506] Psalm 142:3.

[507] Thin Places, November 1, 2009, www.thinplaces.net

[508] Elizabeth Barrett Browning, *Poetry for The Spirit* (London: Watkins, 2006), 280–82.

[509] "Aiden of Lindisfarne," Prayer Foundation, August 15, 2009, http://www.prayerfoundation.org/favoritemonks/favorite_monks_aidan_of_lindisfarne.htm

[510] "Aiden's Prayer," Prayer Foundation, August 15, 2009, http://www.prayerfoundation.org/aidans_prayer.htm

[511] "Brendan the Navigator," Prayer Foundation, August 15, 2009, http://www.prayerfoundation.org/favoritemonks/favorite_monks_brendan_the_navigator.htm

[512] "St. Patrick's Breastplate Prayer," Prayer Foundation, August 15, 2009, http://www.prayerfoundation.org/st_patricks_breastplate_prayer.htm

[513] Deuteronomy 32:11.

[514] The explanation of Genesis 1:2 is best grasped by reading John H. Walton, *The NIV Application Commentary: Genesis* (Grand Rapids: Zondervan), 72–78.

[515] Leon R. Kass, *The Beginning of Wisdom: Reading Genesis* (New York: Free Press, 2003), 29.

[516] George MacDonald, from a sermon preached in June 1882 entitled, "Faith, the Proof of the Unseen."

[517] Romans 8:5.

[518] A. G. Sertillanges, *The Intellectual Life: Its Spirit, Conditions, Methods,* Trans. Mary Ryan (Washington, D.C.: Catholic University of America Press, 1998), 47.

[519] *Ibid.,* 54.

[520] "Career-driven moves fray families' sense of place," *Indianapolis Star* (October 30, 2005).

[521] Michael Pollan, *A Place of My Own: The Education of an Amateur Builder* (New York: Random House, 1997), 51, 41, 39, respectively.

[522] Genesis 1:1.

[523] Genesis 12:1–3; Numbers 13:27; Deuteronomy 19:14, 27:1.

[524] Deuteronomy 20:19.

[525] 2 Chronicles 26:10.

[526] Micah 4:4; Revelation 21:1.

[527] Mark Edmundson, "Dwelling in Possibilities," *The Chronicle of Higher Education* (March 14, 2008).

[528] Peggy Noonan, "The End of Placeness," *The Wall Street Journal* (August 15, 2008).

[529] Susan M. Kelly, "The Sensuous Classroom: Focusing on the Embodiment of Learning," *The Chronicle of Higher Education* (July 25, 2008).

[530] Arthur W. Hunt III, "Cyber Schooling," *Touchstone* (July/August 2013), 17–19.

[531] George Eliot, *Daniel Deronda* (Harmondsworth, 1984), 50.

[532] Genesis 28:14–15; cf. 1 Kings 8:34, 40; 13:34; 14:15; 2 Kings 21:8, 25:21; Nehemiah 10:37.

[533] Ezekiel 36:24–30, 35; cf. Jeremiah 31:33–34; 2 Corinthians 5:17; Hebrews 8:8–12.

[534] Zionsville Fellowship, *Statement of Belief and Practice*, 4, 36, 38.

[535] Revelation 21:1.

[536] Ezekiel 47:1–10.

[537] James R. Akerman and Robert W. Karrow, ed. (Chicago: University of Chicago Press, 2007).

[538] 1 Corinthians 15:47–49; Ephesians 3:14–15.

[539] Genesis 10:5.

[540] Genesis 10:5, 20, 31.

[541] Genesis 10:32; cf. Acts 17:26.

[542] Miles Harvey, *The Island of Lost Maps: A True Story of Cartographic Crime* (New York: G. K. Hall, 2000), 298–91.

543 Gordon R. Lewis and Bruce A. Demarest, *Integrative Theology: Knowing Ultimate Reality, Vol. 1* (Grand Rapids: Zondervan, 1987), 61.

544 Proverbs 25:2 (ESV).

545 Robert L. Allen, *Proverbs: A Commentary on an Ancient Book of Timeless Advice* (Grand Rapids: Baker, 1983), 181.

546 The word "Gnostic" comes from the Greek word for "knowledge." Any Bible dictionary would give background information on the group. After reading descriptions, it becomes clear that Gnostics exist in every culture.

547 Another key Gnostic doctrine maintained that the physical body was bad. The implication clearly attacked the incarnation (coming in flesh) of Christ. First John 1:1–3 and 4:1–6 excoriate the false teaching.

548 In fact, the very next words out of Paul's pen warn of arguments meant to delude Christians.

549 John Eadie, *Colossians* (Grand Rapids: James & Klock, 1977), 181.

550 Johannes P. Louw and Eugene A. Nida, *Greek-English Lexicon of the New Testament Based on Semantic Domains, 2nd ed.* (New York: United Bible Society, 1989), 1:86.

551 Matthew 6:21; 12:35, 52; Luke 12:24, 33–34.

552 H. E. Dana and Julius R. Mantey, *A Manual Grammar of the Greek New Testament* (New York: MacMillan, 1955), 105.

553 Larry Richards, *Expository Dictionary of Bible Words* (Grand Rapids: Zondervan, 1985), 383, 629.

554 Arthur F. Holmes, *Building the Christian Academy* (Grand Rapids: Eerdmans, 2001), 43–44.

555 Abraham Kuyper, 1880, Inaugural Address, Free University of Amsterdam.

556 Desiderius Erasmus, quoted by D. Bruce Lockerbie in *A Passion for Learning: The History of Christian Thought on Education* (Chicago: Moody, 1994), 136.

557 Job 26:14 (NIV).

558 Daniel J. Boorstin, *The Discoverers: A History of Man's Search to Know His World and Himself* (New York: Random House, 1983), 679–83.

CPSIA information can be obtained at www.ICGtesting.com
Printed in the USA
LVOW08s1222110114

368932LV00003B/6/P